MW00328783

SEA OF CALM

GAUTAM SACHDEVA

YogiImpressions®

YogiImpressions®
SEA OF CALM
First published in India in 2020 by
Yogi Impressions LLP
1711, Centre 1, World Trade Centre,
Cuffe Parade, Mumbai 400 005, India.
Website: www.yogiimpressions.com

First Edition, September 2020

Copyright © 2020 by Gautam Sachdeva

All rights reserved. This book may not be reproduced in whole or in part, or transmitted in any form, without written permission from the publisher, except by a reviewer who may quote brief passages in a review; nor may any part of this book be reproduced, stored in a retrieval system, or transmitted in any form or by any means electronic, mechanical, photocopying, recording, or other, without written permission from the publisher.

ISBN 978-93-88677-26-4

RAMESH BALSEKAR
1917-2009

'The beauty of the teaching
lies in its simplicity.
It may not make your life easier,
but it will make it simpler.'

CONTENTS

INTRODUCTION

This book comprises questions and answers culled from talks given by Gautam at his residence in Mumbai and other locations, as well as his answers to emails.

The reader will find that Gautam constantly directs all answers to peace of mind in daily living. The message is always the same, as the teaching is a reflection of the Buddha's famous words: 'Samsara is *dukkha* (misery), Nirvana is *shanti* (peace).'

When Gautam's spiritual guide Ramesh Balsekar used to be asked why he kept saying the same thing again and again in the daily talks he gave at his residence over many years, he replied by saying that the ego, encrusted with years upon years of conditioning, needed constant hammering to break the shell. The words he uttered were new conditioning that could gradually transform the earlier conditioning. In some cases, the transformation could be immediate.

And when he was asked by spiritual seekers and devotees as to why they kept coming back to his satsangs in spite of knowing that he said the same thing day after day, Rameshji replied by saying that the teaching became like one's favourite song, that one loves to hear again and again.

May the simple understanding presented through this teaching guide your boat across the seas of life's journey, through all its ups and downs. And as you, dear reader, go through this book, may you take a dip in the waters of peace.

DAILY LIVING

'To know that you are not living your life but rather, life is being lived through you, by the Source, is living the teaching.'

Can you give some pointers or a sort of checklist that would apply to day-to-day life?

It is actually a very natural process because if you honour 'what is', what comes up in the moment, you will do precisely that which you are meant to do, and so will the other.

Suppose you feel bad about something, 'feeling bad' is a natural aspect of the human experience, for you are not doing it on purpose. If you are sensitive in nature and someone says something that upsets you, the thought that 'I should not be upset' will not arise if there is an understanding that you are made precisely the way God has made you. You would then have a total acceptance of who you are. To fight that natural inclination is, in fact, 'doership'. This is the only pointer—nobody truly does anything.

But since this understanding stays at the intellectual level, all these uncertainties or dilemmas keep cropping up. Everything is precisely as it is, the way God has designed it.

———

Why do you place so much importance on peace of mind?

Rameshji would say, 'What everyone is looking for, whether they know it or not, is peace of mind.' When Ramana Maharshi was asked, 'How does one know whether a sage is a genuine sage?' he replied thus, 'By the degree of peace you feel in his presence and the sense of respect you feel for him.' The Buddha has said, 'Samsara is dukkha. Nirvana is shanti.' So it is not just I who places so much emphasis on peace of mind. It is at the core of all spiritual teachings.

Peace is one's natural state, one's true nature. Almost everyone knows the peace of deep sleep. You don't have to find peace, but rather, strip away that which has got layered and encrusted over it.

―――――――――

Should the goal of life be peace of mind, or an absence of conflict, instead of happiness?

It is happiness through peace of mind that is 'true happiness', not the happiness that depends on pleasure, because pleasures come and go. Life will keep bringing you back to this lesson, until you realise that the happiness that depends on 'something good happening to me' is a cheat. Peace of mind in daily living is true happiness, because this happiness does not depend on something happening to 'you'. Peace of mind, true happiness, is your birthright.

―――――――――

I find peace only when I am alone, away from the city, feeling safe and close to nature. This, however, is very hard to sustain because one needs to earn money to live, and one also desires contact with other human beings. How can this be addressed or dealt with?

Yes, peace is found more easily when one is amidst nature or when one is alone as there are no others to deal with. That is, no other 'egos' to deal with. However, daily living does involve relationships with others—be they friends, relatives or strangers. And peace of mind in daily living is what is desirable and sought, and this is the precious gift of Advaita.

As you have rightly said, one needs to earn money to live and one also desires contact with other human beings. I would encourage you to go back and take another dip in the waters of daily living, rather than isolating yourself, since you have been gifted with this teaching.

The focus of this teaching is on acceptance. Does that mean we are not to reject anything, or is even rejection a part of acceptance?

Even rejection is not your 'doing'. With the light of awareness, the understanding is that everything 'happens'. Rejection was meant to happen, so it happened.

I have a problem of stammering due to which I fear to speak with anyone. I am a medical student who is expected to be a fine speaker. Stammering is leading me to depression. How can I 'accept' my stammering and have peace of mind? I got interested in spirituality after reading 'The Gospel of Sri Ramakrishna'. I have also watched your videos.

'Accepting' your stammering means accepting that it happened because it was God's Will. This does not mean not doing whatever you can to help you with the stammering.

It is only natural that stammering leads to fear and a sense of depression. There are many causes of stammering, and they can be traced by professional psychotherapists as well as speech therapists who can then see how best to help you.

I get bored very easily. Can you say something about this?

Boredom is natural, else one wouldn't get bored. If that is destined to happen, it will happen. Who is it that gets bored? Sit with your boredom for once. Don't avoid it by becoming engaged in other things. One type of boredom is an 'energetic boredom' where the body needs to walk, exercise, and expend energy so that the feeling goes away. But more often than not, boredom is in the mind. And one tries to engage in other activities so that one does not get bored. In a sense, one is running away from just 'being'.

For example, some people have a hard time sitting in meditation with their eyes closed. They get bored. That is because they are habituated to being engaged in something or the other—they are externalised. Then there are others who just close their eyes and are lost to the world. No one gets bored in meditation—it's the mind that gets bored. Why? Because the mind wants to survive, it does not want to die. In meditation it dies.

Real meditation is Consciousness contemplating on Itself. Thoughts are witnessed just like traffic moving by. There is no attachment to these thoughts, which normally translates into thinking. Thoughts will arise, because that is the nature of thoughts. You can't block a thought. Here, thoughts are not the issue, but rather, thinking is. It is the stretching out of a thought in the duration of time that is the issue.

When you're comfortable with just being, you will realise that you don't have to be 'doing' all the time. Boredom could be a sign that the person is habituated to the 'doing' mode all the time. You could not 'do' if you were not conscious. And, as said earlier, meditation is Consciousness contemplating on Itself. Meditation is making one realise that Consciousness is one's true nature.

How do I hold on to the peace I experience in meditation, in the waking state, during my daily routine?
Sri Aurobindo said that it cannot be that spiritual evolution can happen only through meditation, because sitting in meditation is an internal journey while life is mostly about the externals, and therefore—the work becomes the meditation. Daily living is about

working, being engaged during the course of the day, for most people. The point is whether this engagement is a total engagement of the 'working mind', or if one is constantly distracted by the 'thinking mind' that goes into the dead past or an imaginary future. There is a difference.

When one has experienced peace through meditation, the natural desire is for it to permeate one's daily living. But it cannot happen if you want to disconnect from daily living and just be with yourself, at peace while you sit at home in meditation. They must merge, because your life is one expression from birth to death. It is not splintered or compartmentalised into segments such as 'when I work', 'when I am at home', 'when I am in meditation'.

True meditation is living the understanding that God's Will prevails at all times. This means the total acceptance of 'what is', including something you may not like. This includes the total acceptance of people the way God has made them, and the total acceptance of yourself the way God has made you. In other words, the total acceptance that nobody is the 'doer' of their actions— 'God is the Primal Doer'. Living this understanding translates into living a life of peace and equanimity.

―――――――

What should one do to imbibe the teachings in everyday life? There is such a big gap in the teaching I hear and in the life I live; in the choices I make. It is difficult to keep the teachings in your head and to move about engaging in the activities of daily living. Sometimes,

I wonder about what should be guiding me when I make choices and take decisions in my day-to-day life.

It is the teaching that guides you. What the ego does is that it grasps the teaching and makes it a tool with which to start operating your life. This leads to the matter of keeping the teaching in one's head all the time. But this is not needed. Don't do anything. Let the teaching do its work. Just be as you are.

To know that you are not living your life but rather, life is 'being lived' through you, by the Source, is living the teaching. Gradually, this understanding sinks deeper and deeper, during the course of one's daily living, until what was previously an intellectual understanding now settles in the heart.

So the teaching is to just be as you are!

The teaching is that—everything is as it 'Is'. As Ramana Maharshi said, 'Your job is not to be this or that, but to just be.' The teaching is not asking anyone to bring about change as an active process. Transformation happens, change happens, when it, the teaching, starts sinking deeper and deeper.

People would ask Rameshji, 'You keep talking about nobody being the doer of their actions, which we understand intellectually. Nobody including myself is the doer of their actions. But what do I have to do to have the total understanding that I am not the doer?'

Rameshji would answer by saying, 'Have you heard your question?' Your question is, 'What do I have to "do" to have the total understanding that I am "not" the doer?' The answer is very simple and obvious—nothing. If you are not the doer, there is nothing you can do. It can only happen!

It is very difficult to accept that.
Because the ego is designed that way. The ego can even take the ownership of 'non-doership' and use it as a tool. It is not willing to accept that things can happen without its doing.

———————

Everyone is looking for a purpose. How do you do what you are programmed to do, but without looking for validation?
The understanding creates the disengagement. Validation is a need. A need to feel good, to feel important. There is nothing wrong in it, it is a part of the way we are made. The problem is that we 'pursue' validation. This is what drops off, with the understanding. You will no longer be constantly looking for validation, because you know that 'you are not the doer.' That is why the enlightened masters are just being themselves, they are not looking for validation from others. They are living a simple life with peace of mind and equanimity.

It is quite incredible. We can look at everything we do and it will reveal so much to us. But we don't look, because we are too involved and engaged in our drama. This question you have asked is excellent. Now look at your own life and at the situations in which you feel you were looking for validation. Then go deeper, and try and understand why you were looking for validation. You will consistently reach the conclusion that it is because of something you 'did'. When you know that you are not the doer, the constant looking for validation drops.

───────────

My job is very stressful. I wonder whether I should continue working with so much friction. I don't even have a strong ambition as before. I want to pursue something more meaningful, but is this a form of escaping? Any pointers will be helpful.

Yes, what you have described is not just related to work but it is the journey of life, where comfort cannot be found in what happens in life (where there is a lot of 'friction' and suffering) but rather, in one's attitude to life. Then, the purpose of life becomes the living of it.

It is the pressure that dampens the ambition and enthusiasm over the course of time. And the wish arises for a simpler way as this one seems arduous. Or perhaps, a wish to pursue something else that is entirely different.

What should one do in such a situation? The answer lies in the financial dependence on the job. If one is totally dependent on it, then acceptance of 'what is' (including not liking it) brings one to establish a certain peace with the job. If one is not dependent on it, then by all means one can explore the option of pursuing something different as the job is no longer fulfilling.

This brings us to a third scenario—what if one is totally dependent on the job and yet, one cannot function in it anymore? Should one still leave it? What would be the consequences of such a decision? If the job is unbearable and distressing, and could not get any worse, then one could consider leaving it and be open to what the universe has in store. This, of course, takes courage.

In my experience, allowing things to unfold themselves without 'me' taking an active part in the process has been the prudent course of action, as seen in retrospect.

I am a devotee of Shirdi Sai Baba, who lays emphasis on Shraddha (faith) and Saburi (patience).

I have been unemployed for years despite all efforts and keep the faith that one day Sai will bless me with a wonderful opportunity for my desire to be fulfilled. Yet the opportunity never comes and I have huge bills, including my son's education fees, to pay.

Could this be Sai's wish—keeping someone unemployed for years? Is this in my best interests? This, I am unable to understand.

Sorry to hear about your predicament. Peace in such situations can be found only in the acceptance that we could not be placed here unless it was God's Will. And, we can never understand the basis of something so vast and complex as God's Will with the puny human intellect. My teacher Rameshji would say, 'A created object (we) cannot know the will of the Creator (God). A painting can never know why its painter painted it.'

God is the 'Totality of What Is'. True faith is the acceptance that whatever happens, whether we like it or not, is God's Will. In such cases, all we can do is surrender to the will of the Divine, and ask God to give us strength to deal with the challenging situation.

This, according to me, is the deeper meaning of Shraddha and Saburi.

The feeling of separation dissolves, then comes back. Most of the time, the story is one of suffering, or seeking, or fear. Tonight, I resided in the land of peace. Tomorrow is unknown.

Yes, that is exactly the point. No one knows what the next moment brings, sometimes pleasure and sometimes pain. While we have a preference for pleasures inbuilt in us, the running away from pain is what stops with the understanding. It is accepted (and we don't have to like it) as a part of the movement of daily living.

The feeling of separation dissolving and reappearing is what my spiritual teacher referred to as the 'flip-flop'. Nothing can really be 'done' about it, except the witnessing of it. The seeing is the only doing necessary.

Almost everyone's story is one of suffering/seeking/fear. And most of our thoughts are fear-based thoughts. The fact that, as you mentioned, 'The feeling of separation dissolves, then comes back,' and 'Tonight I resided in the land of peace,' means that you have been showered with Grace, without which even this much would not have happened. Why not consider your glass half full and not half empty? Leave it to Grace to open up the heavens for you.

Every session with you has a magical effect and transports me into a different world filled with peace and harmony. This time it felt like I was getting pearls of wisdom, but the joy was short-lived as I misplaced those pearls.

I could see that I get affected and react to everything around, though the teaching literally screams in my ears. It makes me feel that ignorance is bliss and wisdom is misery.

Don't worry about misplacing the pearls; they cannot be. They are not an 'object' that can be misplaced. Let the teaching do its work how and when it is meant to. Sometimes it takes a while for old patterns and conditioning to change or get erased, so to speak. The teaching is fresh conditioning that may alter or transform the earlier conditioning; it is meant to. There are many who are not even aware that they get affected and react to everything around.

Who is it that is aware that they get affected and react to everything around? My spiritual teacher said, 'Consciousness in action is understanding; understanding in action is witnessing.' He did not say that understanding in action is 'doing'.

———————

How can we know ourselves? How can we analyse our journey's progress while we are on it?

There is only one measure—by the degree of peace that you feel. There is no other criteria. And it is the job of the thinking mind to take one away from that peace. The thinking mind, which is the ego with a sense of 'doership', is very good at that. The moments of deep peace that you feel are something to be so grateful for, because many people don't feel that. But the mind tends to only focus on the moments when you do not feel at peace. That is the nature of the thinking mind. To ask questions after questions after questions. That is why I say, thank God for your deep sleep.

How can we erase/clear a painful memory?

Who created memory? Did you create it? Memory is a part of the mechanics of the human brain. You cannot erase memory. You would not be alive without memory. For example, once you put your hand in the fire, you immediately withdraw it lest it burn your hand. Now, the memory serves you well to know not to put your hand in the fire again. During the course of one's life, there are moments of pleasure and moments of pain that get registered in the memory. The remembrance of pleasures makes us want more of them, and the remembrance of pain makes us fearful that they might arise again. This, then, becomes the burden of memory; the burden of our conditioning through which we view life.

To clear a painful memory is to accept it; to accept that it happened because it was God's Will. The memory does not go away, but all the compulsive thinking associated with it does. A large part of painful memories are based on what we feel someone has done to us, or what we have done to someone. When we accept that no one truly does anything and that God is the only doer, then the painful memory does not get cleared, but is healed.

A painful memory makes us feel sad. The memory does not allow one to disengage from thoughts of the pain felt, and this in turn hinders one's capacity to work in daily life. It is futile to try and disengage from thoughts of pain, push them aside or brush them under the carpet. If you try to disengage, you are in fact, creating further engagement and strengthening the memory by resisting it. You are adding to the original burden of the memory.

The end of 'doership' is the end of that additional burden. The end of considering others or oneself as the doer is the end of blame, condemnation, malice, hatred, jealousy, envy, pride, arrogance, guilt, shame, and so on. When the mind no longer carries this load, it stops going into an imaginary future or the dead past, and then one rests in 'being'.

If a button was pressed and your entire memory wiped out, what would be left? The sense of being. You would still know that you exist, but you would not know anything beyond that. But right now, the person who does not want the memory is still there and is asking the question. If that person were not there, who will be left to enjoy the absence of memory? Even the question would not arise.

When a deer sees a lion, it is afraid and automatically runs away. Isn't the deer afraid of death?

Of course it is. The deer is programmed to be afraid of biological death, so it runs.

Well, so am I!

No. You ask questions, which the deer does not. The deer does not live in fear—the fear of the future. Unlike you, it does not think, 'What's going to be my bank balance three years from now?' … and so on. The biological fear of death in a human being is that which does not make you close your eyes and cross the road. That is what is common between the deer and a human being. But we have a psychological problem with dying. We have the intellect that God gave us, which makes us ask questions. The deer has no questions to ask. The deer does not want possessions; it does not build a monumental story around another deer it falls in love with—'Will you be with me for the rest of my life?'—nor does it indulge in other such projections.

But the deer also falls in love and has children …

That's a natural, biological process—pure being. The deer does not seek permanency in the future.

What about nomads?

They're probably more 'awakened' than most of us. They don't get attached to places and things. They simply move on. We get habituated even to the restaurants we go to, and the table we sit at. *(Laughter)*

If one's conditioning leads one to do harm to oneself and others, but Advaita says not to fight the conditioning, is this one's karma/destiny?

I don't think it is a question of 'fighting' the conditioning, which perhaps is something you might have been doing through your spiritual practices. I repeat, Advaita brings to awareness that your actions are a result of your genes and conditioning, over neither of which you have any control. This makes it easier to accept others, as well as yourself, for who they or you are. Acceptance of 'what is' makes one see things in a clearer, impersonal light. This awareness, and how deeply it sinks in (even if initially only at the intellectual level), can itself change, alter or transform the current conditioning. Who is the one concerned with 'fighting' the conditioning? It's the ego, of course, which can only do things like 'fight', as it derives its sense of self from that very activity.

Destiny is 'what is' in the moment. And one never knows what the next moment brings. Why project the past into the future and wonder whether that's your destiny? It is the thinking mind which tends to do that. Why assume you may do harm to yourself or others as part of your destiny, based on past experience? Let God decide that.

My guru would always say to seekers who came to visit him, 'Why consider your glass half empty? Consider it half full. If God has brought you here so far, why think that He will drop you here?' Perhaps you need to take a break from trying to de-condition yourself, and let life flow with the new perspective you have gained.

Further, if there is a deep understanding, then the issue of harming others will not arise. If there is the deep understanding that it is the same Consciousness that functions through all of us, where is the question of harming someone for something they are supposed to have 'done'?

That is all I have to offer for now. May you rest in the warm embrace of the teaching.

––––––––––

I do find the peace, the timeless dimension, but I suffer for the hatred man has towards man. I hate the war machine. I can't or perhaps don't want to stop my apparent suffering when I see that a few people in high places pit man against man. I know this isn't acceptable in the non-dual arena but I can't stand this division in one family. I hate this.

It's quite natural to hate the 'war machine' … you could call it hate arising in the moment. Even this is God's Will. If one is sensitive (based on one's genes and conditioning) then one cannot bear such insensitivities that humans inflict on one another. This reaction is not 'your' reaction, as it were. It is a 'happening' that had to happen.

The total acceptance of 'what is', includes the acceptance of one's reaction to 'what is'. And we needn't like 'what is'. This is where the peace is to be found.

––––––––––

I was brought up by a father who was an alcoholic and also abusive, and a mother who passively went along with the state of affairs. Growing up, I learnt the patterns of my mother's and father's conduct/ behaviour, and continued to act out various patterns until my early 30s when life seemed to stop working for me: relationships broke

*down, jobs did not work out, I felt angry, depressed, empty, alone.
I am now 38 years of age and I have been working on my emotional
and psychological health, and my spiritual understanding. But
I am tired, very tired, of the therapy, yoga classes, health treatments,
healers, etc. I seem to oscillate between the stress and work of
trying to de-condition myself, and the unhealthy ways of thinking
and acting that seem to be the default. I can understand that.
'Self-improvement' can be an exhausting process.*

Indeed, that was your childhood conditioning over which you
had no control, and neither did your father or mother, over their
conditioning. That is the Advaita perspective.

At a talk given by me last year, a man told me that he had tried
various healings and therapies—reiki, pranic healing, workshops,
courses, and so on, and that he was quite a spiritual tourist in that
sense. He wondered if and when this would stop, since he had
been at it for over 20 years.

My answer was simple. I said that it would stop the moment
he asked himself what he was looking for. Once he knew that,
then at least he would know whether he found it. He was quite
astonished. He said he did not know what he was looking for, and
even the thought of it had not arisen.

Then, I repeated what my guru used to say—'What the
human being is looking for deep down, and whether he knows
it or not, is peace of mind.' The fact that he was continuing to
'look around' meant that he had not found that elusive peace of
mind. This teaching impacted him (*the member of the audience*)

tremendously as he wholeheartedly agreed that it was peace of mind that he was looking for. He now knows that there is a 'criteria' and he needn't look around aimlessly.

Sometimes, one has the good fortune of chancing upon the teaching of Advaita, which in my experience is capable of bestowing this peace. You have said that it resonates deeply within you. That is because it validates your life experience.

We did not create our childhood conditioning in the first place, and yet we get involved in endless efforts to de-condition our conditioning. It is ironic, but that is the way the ego functions—in a mode based on 'doership'. Advaita offers a unique perspective in its understanding. This is what is meant by 'don't fight one's conditioning'. When it is clearly seen that we are all shaped by our genes and conditioning, both of which are not in our control, then how can we blame others (and more importantly, ourselves) for something they or we are supposed to have done?

We are all instruments through whom God's Will functions. When this realisation sinks deeper and deeper, it is observed that one's conditioning gets transformed over a period of time; at times it may get transformed instantly. So rather than 'doing' something to de-condition oneself, it is in fact the understanding that starts working through you, in daily living. This, in turn, creates fresh conditioning and it is reflected in one's attitude and response to current situations. All we need to 'do' is to give it a chance. In other words, your resonance with Advaita is the new conditioning that brings you the peace.

Although the teaching has impacted my daily living tremendously, there are times when I just can't follow them and it somehow makes me feel like a failure. At times, this failure overpowers me and at other times, I just let it be. All these years, I have been living for others and never really cared about myself or my feelings or what I really want. I guess it's the conditioning. Finally I have started to think a bit about myself and what I really want, which has led me to your doorstep. Now all I seek is peace with myself and within me.

It's very rare that I can be me, it's more like I am playing a role with a mask on, every day. It's only with a few handful of people that I can be me. I have no idea if it's an insecure feeling or some kind of fear.

I have to tell you that when I entered your living room for the satsang, my monkey mind just switched off automatically and I was totally blank, and it was like this for almost 3-4 days. I enjoyed this state of mind but now, it has all gone out of the window. I can literally laugh and cry about it.

Please do share some thoughts on how I can keep walking on this path, and 'live' each and every moment of Advaita in my daily life. I want to live 'now' and can't be bothered about what's next or tomorrow.

'Failure' is one of the favourite words of the ego, with its sense of 'doership'. It implies—'I failed to do something I should have.' Neither success nor failure are yours, but rather, movements in consciousness. But the ego loves these words, as it then knows who or what it is; it has an identity.

My suggestion is to focus less on these labels and let life flow. We all have good days and not-so-good days. Everything needn't be perfect, according to our idea of what 'perfection' is. As you mention, 'There are times I just can't follow the teachings and it somehow makes me feel like a failure.' This is the flip-flop. All that needs to be 'done', so to speak, is to witness it. This is what is happening in any case—as you say, 'At times this failure overpowers me totally and at times, I just let it be.' Even this is not in your control.

When you say you wear a mask, you are speaking on behalf of most of humanity. The mask is the ego with its identifications … an image we project so we may be accepted or liked, as we are afraid that if people see who we truly are, we will not be liked. This too needs to be just seen for what it is.

———————

Please tell me, if I see myself enlightened in a dream, does this mean something?

Dreams are generally psychological reactions to the waking state. If, for example, enlightenment is very much on your mind, then it could appear as a dream (as this is your aspiration). Or if the dream is a prophetic one, then perhaps enlightenment can happen if it's destined to.

All in all, it is a nice dream to have, though still a dream!

RELATIONSHIPS

'The understanding that there is
no other, but only Consciousness,
transforms relationships.'

As a mother, what should I do when my child is doing something wrong? Should I not stop the child, or should I just let him do it because he is a child of God, and therefore doing precisely what God wants him to do?

You should do exactly that which you, as a parent, think and feel you should do. It is quite natural, as you only want to protect your child and ensure that he or she grows up with the right values and principles. However, telling or sharing your point of view is quite different from enforcing your point of view, which of course needs to be done sometimes. Invariably, parents fall into the trap of relentless domination and control, and then the standard parent-child drama plays out. In shamanic traditions, this process is called 'domestication'.

During our growing up years, our mother never told us the word 'No'. She would just tell us the pros and cons of a situation, but would never stop us from doing anything. And we—my sisters and I—all grew up so disciplined; it was quite amazing.

Parents need to realise that children come with their own destinies.

My aunt has pancreatic cancer and it is spreading fast. Meanwhile, my uncle has been diagnosed with a brain tumour but thankfully he appears to be stable after angioplasty. I feel completely helpless and afraid. It all seems to have come at once, and we really do not know what to do. Witnessing the suffering of our much loved aunt is unbearable.

Our loved one's suffering is surely unbearable, but any form of suffering anyone is going through is unbearable to witness. This is simply because we ourselves know what suffering is.

The point is that we don't suffer fully. When we are in a helpless situation, we compound the suffering by conceptualising—'Why did this happen to me?', 'What did I do wrong?', 'Things should not have been this way!', 'My aunt should not be suffering!', 'The doctors are to blame!', 'Why is God being so cruel to me?', and so on.

What is supposed to be pure suffering, because there is no way out, becomes compounded because there is a 'me' that is now involved in the suffering. Suffering has to be accepted when there is no choice, but we try to find a way out of the suffering, to escape it, even though we are not given that option.

Some things in life must be endured. We have to accept this. There is nothing wrong in suffering, in crying, in feeling low. It is the thinking mind that actually gives sustenance to the fire of suffering. And so the answer to this question about what you can do because you have two family members who are ailing, is truly nothing but to create space for the acceptance of 'what is', including your reaction to it. That is where the peace is to be found. The peace is not to be found in trying to find a way out of the suffering. It is to be found 'through' the suffering, knowing that it happened because it had to happen. This is why the Buddha said, 'Samsara is dukkha. Nirvana is shanti.'

On a lighter note, it was Advaita sage Sri Nisargadatta Maharaj who once said, '82 years ago my parents enjoyed for a few minutes and after that I had to suffer for 82 years!' What he was trying to point at is that life is imprisonment, but we convert simple imprisonment into rigorous imprisonment. How? By blame, condemnation, guilt, shame, arrogance, pride, hatred, malice, envy, jealousy, based on what somebody 'did' to us or what we 'did' to somebody.

So the question is, 'Is this imprisonment going to be a simple imprisonment or a rigorous imprisonment?' Is it a pessimistic view of life? Not really, because everyone has experienced suffering in some form or another in their lifetime. Almost everyone will say that they have seen more downs than ups in their lives. As Lord Buddha said to a woman—whose child had died and who requested the Buddha to revive her—'Find me a house in which nobody has died, and get some food from there to help me revive the child.' Of course, she could not find such a house as everyone had lost someone or the other. She then realised the inevitability of death and thanked the Buddha for this compassionate lesson. So, 'acceptance' is truly what gives peace of mind.

When people would raise this very subject with my spiritual teacher, and ask questions like—'Why me?', 'Why did this happen to my family member?', 'I have not harmed anyone ever, so why do I have to go through this?'—Rameshji would reply, 'A painting can never know why the painter painted it.' So who is asking the question? The individual—the ego with its sense of 'doership'—is wanting to know something about something that has happened according to the will of the Creator. 'A created object can never know the will of the Creator Subject,' as he would say.

Or again, as he would say, 'People ask, "Why has God created handicapped children? What harm have they done to anyone?" But then, nobody asks God, "Why has God created healthy children?" You see, we take it for granted.' When there is a problem, we say it should not be this way. But life is duality. Up and down, black and white, left and right, rich and poor, healthy children and handicapped children, health and disease, and so on. Accepting the basic duality of life brings a sense of peace and equanimity.

———————

When I hire staff and they turn out to be very good performers, I do not take the credit for it. But if they turn out to be troublesome, I take the blame and feel guilty about how I could have made this error in judgement. Why so?

If a child who is running around the house knocks down an expensive item, let's say a curio lying on a table in the living room, he is scolded by the parent. As far as the parent is concerned, the child 'did' something as a result of which he is reprimanded. This is how the sense of 'doership' gets ingrained in the child. However, while the child was running around all the time and didn't knock something down, the child wasn't appreciated and told, 'Congratulations, you did not drop anything!'

So when the child becomes an adult, if something goes wrong, he takes ownership of it because that has been the conditioning in the formative years. However, if there was an understanding—deep down on the part of the parent—that neither knocking down an item nor not knocking down an item are 'done' by the child, but rather it is a 'happening' that has occurred, then the conditioning of the child would be entirely different.

What's more, the reaction of the parent depends on the value of the item, because it is the adult who has invested in the item, not the child. For the child, it is just one object out of many in the child's universe, so to speak. If it is an expensive item, the reaction of the parent may be more severe than if it is inexpensive.

If there is the total understanding that nobody truly does anything, then one will not blame others and one will not blame or condemn oneself. Even our parents were conditioned by their parents. When we say that nobody truly 'does' anything, it means everything is simply happening. But we take control and ownership of everything and we say, 'He did this', 'He did that', and 'I did this' and 'I did that'. That is where the suffering begins.

What's important to note is that this is part of the Divine hypnosis, 'the *leela*' (God's game). It was meant to be this way, as part of our human nature. This sense of 'doership' is not something that we created on our own; this is the game of life, and over time we realise that deep down, nobody truly does anything because it is God, Consciousness, which is the Primal Doer. We do not live our lives but rather, life is 'being lived' through us. We are 'being lived', by the Source.

Eckhart Tolle's teachings have changed my life and I feel like I am finally leaving the prison that used to be my complete identification with my thoughts and old patterns. Although I am extremely grateful for everything, I have had some difficulty as I am 20 years old, and now more than ever, I am having trouble relating to people my age. I have different interests now because of my desire for peace, and it seems to me that all that my friends want to do is to get drunk every day. I would be deeply grateful for any words you could share with me that could help me through this difficult situation.

20 years old is quite young to have this level of awareness itself, which is wonderful. But the whole point is that life—daily living—is about one's relationship with others, whether they are your family members, colleagues, friends, the stranger you meet or even the beggar on the road. Harmonious relationships lead to peace of mind in daily living. In other words, this means—to be comfortable with others and to be comfortable with oneself.

Or, to put it differently, not to be uncomfortable with others and not be uncomfortable with oneself.

Now, you feel that over time your understanding of life—the prism through which you view it—is changing, based on the teachings you have come across, the books you have read, a spiritual master you have met, and so on.

What happens is that sometimes you cannot relate to a particular set of people who were in your life earlier or might still be, because there is a shift in your own awareness and understanding.

It now might just be social conditioning over the formative years that makes you hold on to those relationships. Or. It now might be clear to you that you do not want to be with the same set of friends anymore, as you no longer derive a sense of self from those old relationships. You may feel, 'I have new interests now, which are not shared by this old set.'

The point is to accept that they too are on their own journey, as planned by the Divine. There is no judgement or resentment about them and their activities. They are who they are, how God—the Source, made them, in the social structure and context God has placed them in. In other words, there is no higher ground taken by you to stand on as a result of a comparison with them.

As far as you are concerned, your conditioning has now been transformed in a certain way, how the Divine has planned it, so you move on as it is time for you to move on. You perhaps might get a new set of friends over time. But when there is a full acceptance of people for who they are, then the relationship is harmonious because we are not saying, 'I don't like who they are now, therefore I am moving away from them.' It's just that that vibration does not resonate with who you are today.

On another note, even a person's getting drunk every day is nothing but a relationship. It is the relationship of that person with alcohol. Earlier we were speaking of a relationship with people. Here it is a relationship with alcohol. In fact, it is not really their relationship with alcohol, but rather, it is their relationship with what they feel on account of consuming the alcohol.

The point is that nobody is doing anything deliberately, as such. When there is pain and suffering in the formative years, sometimes one takes to alcohol to suppress that; to suppress the pain carried by the identified 'me'. That is why it is said that after having a few drinks, some people are able to express themselves more. It looks like they are having fun, but it only appears that way for a brief period of time.

All in all, one need not feel guilty about not wanting to meet one's old friends anymore. The guilt will arise if you feel you are 'doing' something by withdrawing, but if you allow it to flow naturally, the river takes you away from where you are not meant to be, and you will flow in the direction it is taking you towards. So like we used to say in our school days, 'Go with the flow like H$_2$O.' That's it!

Accept others for who they are, accept yourself for who you are, that is all. There is no thought about how people should be; that is where the problem comes in. Then there are those who even give free advice—'You should be like this', 'You should not behave like that', and so on. Especially those on the spiritual path give free advice because they think they know better, because they feel that their way is the right way.

My family and friends follow other paths. They do not respond positively to my inclination towards this path. They are continuing with their old patterns. Many times there is quite a bit of entanglement and drama. How does one come to terms with this situation? Simply by understanding that they are operating through their own blueprint, their own conditioning. That is their life's journey. You are concerned with your own journey. You have two options. One is, if you are dependent socially on their company (we are all creatures of social dependence; that is why we keep certain friendships in place, have certain projections, and so on), if you are still deriving a sense of self from some friendships, you keep those friendships. The other option is to wish them well and move on, if they no longer resonate with you. You may find yourself getting a new set of friends over time. But do not judge them. They are precisely the way God has made them, just as you are precisely the way God has made you.

Now, family relationships are hard-wired, karmic relationships. In some instances, the relationship is not harmonious. What the spiritually aware family member brings to the relationship is—a witnessing presence. You are no longer in a reactive pattern which you used to be engaged in earlier, perhaps right from childhood. If you are no longer giving sustenance to that back and forth action-reaction loop, the other family member will realise that the harder they try, the lesser the reaction will come back from you. This eventually causes a break in the cycle of reactivity. Reaction comes from the sense of 'doership'—he 'did' this to me, or I 'did' this to him. If the sense of 'doership' is absent in either one, then there is little or no resistance. That (the witnessing presence) tends to throw people off.

One should constantly repeat the mantra, 'This too shall pass.' Everything in our field of consciousness is impermanent; we ourselves are impermanent. It is like a dream. So while our problems are real in the waking state, the understanding that our lives, as well as all events that take place during our lifetime, are transient, changes the way one views situations as well as relationships.

———————

Why is there love in a relationship and still much suffering? What is Rnanubandhan? You keep mentioning it.

There is love in relationships because our very nature is love. Our nature is love because Consciousness is love. It is the same Consciousness operating through all of us, just as it is the same electricity that runs through all the gadgets in the kitchen.

The ancient Indian masters would expound on the concept of Rnanubandhan. The closest translation would be, 'the debt of a former relationship'. The concept of rebirth is emphasised in Indian scriptures. So some teachings point to this—the biggest problems or the biggest troublemakers in your life are on account of a cosmic debt which predates this (current) incarnation. And that is why the sages would refer to this cause-effect or action-reaction loop that is prevalent in relationships. The Aghori Vimalananda said, 'Effect is cause revealed, cause is effect concealed.' You cannot have one without the other.

This alludes to the meaning of karma. Karma means 'action'. Action and reaction, which goes on and on. So according to this concept, your strongest 'bandhans', or bonds, are the ones which are here to teach you the deepest lessons.

Many people have that one relationship in life which really gets them down; either someone has cheated them of money or someone is antagonizing them or is emotionally blackmailing them, and so on. That is the 'rna' operating. Now, what is the way out of this? The only way out is when you have the understanding that it is not the 'individual' doing it to you. Once you stop blaming someone or condemning someone, the 'rna' starts breaking up because you have the total acceptance that in the bigger picture, it is the 'Cosmic Law' and God's Will that is operating. God is the only doer and we are all instruments of the Divine.

Again, according to the Indian scriptures, after realisation there is no rebirth. Why? Because there is no 'rna' left. The sense of 'doership' is totally annihilated. Ramana Maharshi would say that whatever is happening is on account of *prarabdha karma*, which means the past karma. It just appears in this lifetime that we are doing something and something happens. There is so much we don't understand, but we try our best to make sense of things, analyse and overinterpret situations, but the force of God's Will and how it operates is beyond the understanding of our puny human intellect. One needs to realise that one's intellect is indeed very limited. It is not about linear thinking and formulas—'Okay so this happened, therefore the result is that this will happen ...' and so on. That kind of dialogue is the antics of the thinking mind, going into the dead past or projecting itself into an imaginary future, dissecting reality as a 'whole'. Many things that happen simply don't make sense; that has been everyone's experience.

And so, in a relationship, when there is this understanding that no one is a doer of their actions, the same patterns are no longer repeated. The masters are here to guide us, the teaching is here to guide us, and if it is in one's destiny, relationships get redefined and thus become harmonious. Then one's only bond is with the 'Lord', the 'Source', 'Consciousness'. That's it. Therefore, to answer your question, the suffering is there because of the Rnanubandhan, and with the dawn of understanding, the relationship gets healed to one of love, so to speak. Not a personal love between two individuals, but rather, a love prevalent despite the limitations of the person. My teacher Rameshji would say, 'Love is the absence of separation and separation is the absence of love.'

———

When someone antagonizes us, what should we do?

Once again, do precisely that which you think and feel you should do. We have the choice of either staying there, discussing the matter with the antagonizer, explaining our perspective to him or her, and if all that has failed, then walking away. When the pain inflicted in the relationship cannot be borne beyond a point, then the better option might be to walk away.

What many of us do is to stay in that relationship because we derive an identity from that, and we complain and complain. That is why teachers like Eckhart Tolle say that once you accept 'what is', then stop complaining about it, or walk away. But to be in a situation and to complain about it non-stop—that is what creates trouble for us. A second layer of suffering thus gets added on to the original suffering, making matters worse.

I know somebody whose life is a complaint from morning to evening. She is the daughter of a millionaire. She either has a problem with her friend, or mother, or servant, the chaos of Mumbai, the weather, and so on. It is like a living, complaining machine. It is a mind—not at peace.

What is the place of compassion in this teaching?

Compassion is a natural outcome of living the teaching. One feels compassionate for another, as the sense of separation diminishes. One feels compassionate because one now knows that we are all a brotherhood of instruments through whom God's Will functions.

Compassion arises naturally in a sage. The sage knows that it is a person's destiny to go through what he or she is going through, because that is their journey of life. So what does the sage bring to the equation? The sage brings his presence and peace. The sage does not go about getting involved in all his disciples' problems, with a view to solve them. True compassion does not mean getting involved in every situation and everyone's problems. True compassion is a feeling of 'oneness', when all judgements and analyses undertaken by the thinking mind are set aside, and one 'feels' for someone, and for what they are going through.

It is important to note that true compassion is spontaneous. Many of us want to be appreciated and loved, so that's what motivates us to do something for people and to help them out. That is also an egoic need. You can just be there for someone. You need not do anything. You just have to listen to them and be there for them. That is what the wise ones do. They do not make a transaction out of compassion.

———

There are human beings who truly do not have a conscience. My whole life has been the story of two such people. In fact, they are the ones responsible for my spiritual journey; their inhumanity pushed me towards God.

If such a person is harming innocent children in the ways he disciplines them, through harsh punishments, yelling, controlling, etc., how do I sit back and meditate in this painful environment?

Do I continue to meditate on the fact that this world is an illusion, that everything is happening according to the Divine plan, and that the little child has come with his/her own karma and fate, therefore, I need not do anything?

I can get involved in a more worldly way and contact therapists, and maybe report the matter to the authorities. However, I am so far into my enlightenment journey that I feel torn about getting involved. I believe that God does everything and I think I have fully surrendered. However, I have got completely shaken to the core. The fear is grabbing me so badly, there are no words to describe it.

Is this mental suffering going to finally lead me to enlightenment, since it is too much to bear?

Firstly, if you think you have surrendered, then you haven't. True surrender is the absence of the 'me' which thinks it has surrendered.

With the understanding, you do precisely what you think and feel you should do in a given situation, and then leave the results to God's Will. For example, if you feel you need to report a matter to the police or go to a therapist, you must honour that feeling and act upon it. No one else can decide this for you. To use the teaching not to take action is what the ego can sometimes do. Where taking an action comes naturally, not to take action becomes 'doership'.

Action becomes all the more important as we live in a society with rules and regulations. That is the reason why we have systems to report criminal offences.

Regarding one's inherent nature, I often use the example

that my spiritual teacher Rameshji gave in his talks. It involved a documentary that appeared on television decades ago, showing whales being slaughtered. Two very famous people saw this programme. One was a Hollywood star and the other was the famous Indian philosopher J. Krishnamurti. The Hollywood star decided to do something about it as she had the financial resources as well as fame, and so started a movement to save the whales. On the other hand, Krishnamurti saw the same programme and being of a gentle and timid disposition, could not bear to see the suffering of the animals. So, he switched off the TV. Each one acted according to their nature.

The journey of enlightenment is not separate, as such, from one's circumstances. All aspects of life and living are included in this journey. Similarly, meditation as a practice is of no use if it does not permeate one's daily living. It is not necessary that mental suffering should lead to enlightenment—in many cases it leads to more mental suffering. Enlightenment will happen if it is destined to happen. To work towards getting enlightenment is no excuse for not taking action where one feels it is required.

––––––––––

I have been married for 12 years, with two children. On multiple occasions, my wife has asked me for a divorce. I have tried my best to give her whatever she asked for but I can see that it's failing. She blames me for her suffering and misery. I don't know what I am doing wrong or where I am making a mistake.

I try to calm her down and ask her to think about the kids. I have compromised at every level so as to simply keep my family intact. I just don't understand what else I can do to hang on to this meaningless relationship.

It seems clear that your wife wants a divorce, but you are reluctant to grant it for the valid reasons you have mentioned. And of course, she has her reasons too, which would be equally valid for her.

Sometimes relationships don't work out in spite of our best efforts—this has to be accepted with grace too, as part of God's Will. All we can do is try our best in such situations, but the results are not in our control. However, to force a situation or relationship to work beyond a point is also not healthy. And it brings pain to all concerned. In such instances, trusting the universe and moving on is the best option.

I am not a relationship expert and perhaps you need counselling by a therapist to take you through this difficult time you are facing, mentally and emotionally. These teachings are not a substitute for professional advice.

What do I do when a parent is in extreme pain? It just reminds me that Advaita has not sunk in yet, in my daily living. I also understand that I cannot artificially do that, but I need to know primarily how I can make the parent feel better and maybe get some peace of mind myself as well. I would probably be strong if it were my own personal pain, but how can I see my parent in this situation?

The understanding of Advaita cannot make pain disappear. When a parent is in pain, it is bound to be painful for their children too. That's the natural flow of life. To accept that pain is a part of life—and feeling the pain when a loved one is in pain and knowing that there is not much one can do about it—is what our experience of life is about. It is the non-acceptance that brings on the additional layer of suffering, over that of the original pain.

Peace of mind is to be found in knowing that you did all that you could, to alleviate your parent's pain and to provide them with as much comfort as possible.

This acceptance of the 'will' of the Divine, even though it's painful in such cases, gives the strength one needs to live one's life courageously. This is why Maharaj said that acceptance, and not running away from pain, is an important step in the journey of liberation.

———————

Despite the intellectual understanding that we are all instruments of God, we have to deal with others according to their behaviour. For instance, I do get angry at some people. Can you please shed some light on this?

Of course, you have to do exactly what you think you should do in a particular situation as well as in a relationship. But now, when your overriding thought is that this person is precisely the way he/she has been made by God, it removes the sting from the relationship. The finger-pointing stops, for now you know everyone acts on the basis of their nature, that is, their genetics and conditioning. Then you do what you need to do. If you have to express your point of view, you will do so and the usual mechanics of daily living take over. But you will not go to sleep with thoughts of hatred, malice, blame, condemnation and so on, all based on what someone 'did' to you. That mental dialogue is erased. And that is when one knows that the intellectual understanding has sunk into the heart.

It is natural that anger may arise on the spur of the moment, in a given situation. It is a part of being human. But what we do is, we hold onto that anger and we make a story out of it. What was spontaneous anger in the moment gets stretched in the duration of time, and we now get 'involved' in the anger. This then colours our thinking, and therefore, how we view the relationship. It is now 'my anger'.

How do I give this understanding and the peace it brings, to my parents? They worry unnecessarily. I try to talk to them but it does not help.

Your intentions are noble in that you would like to explain to your parents how this understanding has given you peace and equanimity in daily living. But all you can do is try; the results are in God's hands. One need not try too hard to give this understanding to people. If one has a vibration of peace, then others sense it and sometimes that is what in turn makes them peaceful. So it's not necessarily a process of words and telling people things.

To be at peace is a gift that gives of itself; it doesn't need 'you' to give peace to others. Just like it is the nature of the sun to shine. How can the sun give sunlight? It doesn't have to 'give' sunlight. Its very nature is to emit rays of light.

To be at peace is to give peace. It is not an object to be given. There is no question of giving peace to others because peace is one's nature. If you are peaceful by nature your presence will radiate peace. You do not acquire peace and then give what you have acquired.

The sun does not make the distinction of who will receive its light and who will not; that is how it is when one is peaceful. There is no differentiation in the people around you because it has got nothing to do with them. Your light of peace is shining upon everything and everyone that you see and come in contact with.

Everyone is on the same journey, and all will eventually reach their destination. We need not struggle to control or influence the journey of our parents or our loved ones. What is meant to happen, will happen, when it is meant to.

NON-DOERSHIP

'What sustains action and reaction
is the sense of doership.'

In your videos, you appear so calm and still, and I aspire to be there and awaken the Guru within with God's grace, but wanted to understand your journey to this state of being?

There was nothing I 'did' to be calm and still. It simply happened as a part of the evolution of my spiritual journey. As a child, I had a calm and timid disposition. Your aspiration is a noble one, and to have this aspiration is a gift you have been given. Allow Grace to lead the way to its fulfilment.

———————

I resonate with the teachings of 'non-doership' and that the outcomes of actions are God's Will. In my personal experience, when one is calm and acts, then it's easier to accept the outcome as one hasn't reacted per se but has thought and acted. But when in an emotionally charged situation, one reacts and the outcome is not ideal, then how does one remove the 'doership' aspect from one's reaction? Isn't the reaction under the individual's control? Sometimes we as humans, despite knowing that it's not right to react, still do.

Ultimately, the reaction is not under the individual's control. There are too many factors that determine a reaction. Perhaps he or she had a stressful day, some bad news earlier in the day, erratic hormone levels, blood pressure, and so on—the list could be endless. This is all in addition to one's conditioning and genetics, over which no one has had any control. And your next sentence, 'Sometimes we as humans, despite knowing that it's not right to react, still do,' proves this very point.

Let's say something is the consequence of the reaction, then how does one understand that this was God's Will? How does one remove the sense of 'doership' from the reaction? One feels regret for it later as it was still one's own response to something in life.
All actions and reactions have consequences. It is all God's Will. When the understanding dawns that it was not 'my' reaction, the sense of 'doership' is removed. Regret may certainly arise and could also lead to an apology, but there is no guilt or shame.

———————

I have been reading Eckhart Tolle's 'The Power of Now' and I have been practicing being 'present'. I am being vigilant of the mind as much as possible. Every time I catch it going into the past or the future, I do try to remain 'present' but it is extremely difficult to maintain that vigilance all the time. It gets very frustrating because you practice it for a few moments and then the mind is again running back into the past or the anxiety builds up about the future. How do I make myself stay more in the present moment?
The issue here is 'I am vigilant'. The vigilance or heightened awareness is not yours, it is simply there. When the heightened

awareness is there, you are in the 'now'; when it slips away, you are not in the 'now'. But what happens is that the ego comes in and says, 'I am vigilant. How could I slip away from that vigilant position?' And so it becomes very frustrating for the ego, because the ego took ownership of the vigilance.

Vigilance is there in the first place because the thinking mind, that runs into the dead past or an imaginary future, is absent. So when one is in the 'now', the thinking mind is not functioning. So, to say 'I am vigilant' is not accurate because you have claimed ownership of the vigilance, which in fact is the absence of the very 'you' that claims ownership. When you no longer do that (claim that you are vigilant), you will realise that vigilance is sometimes there and sometimes not, but the frustration is reduced because it is no longer 'me' who is doing this entire exercise and attempting to be in the 'now'.

The ownership of the 'me' is the problem; it claims ownership of everything. In this instance, it is vigilance. And once you relax into this understanding, you will realise that sometimes you are in the present moment, sometimes you are not in the present moment. Even if the frustration at not being present arises, which is natural, you will not claim the frustration as well; it will be like a pure frustration. So the overall anxiety which the ego builds up by claiming, 'I am not vigilant', 'I am frustrated', is what starts getting corrected. We need to leave things to be as they are.

Let this process of flip-flop take its own course, without getting entangled in this whole thing about—'How could I have been vigilant eight out of ten times, but failed twice?' I received a mail from a girl who was deeply impacted by *The Power of Now*. She said that for 12 years she had her anger under control thanks to the book, but one day when she fought with her boyfriend in the car, she got out and slammed the door shut. And she said, 'There went my 12 years of being in the now!' She then wondered what the point of all those 12 years of practice was, if it was reduced to this one incident of getting angry.

All I said was, 'Look, these things happen. It is okay. We are all not Buddhas sitting here. It happens that one was composed for 12 years and then one lost that composure after 12 years. We have to drop that constant need to claim our position, 'I was composed', 'I was not composed', and so on.

Vigilance is a good word you used because, truly, vigilance is heightened awareness. A surgeon, when he is conducting an operation, is vigilant. It is his 'working mind' in operation at the time, in the 'now'. But if he starts thinking about what would happen if the surgery doesn't go well (let's say the patient being operated upon is a big politician), then it is his thinking mind that becomes active, for he is now thinking of an imaginary future that may or may not come to pass.

Therefore, to sum up, vigilance is the absence of the 'me' with its sense of 'doership', which is the thinking mind. So it is like an elephant pit—one that it has dug for itself—that the 'me' is falling into when it says, 'I am vigilant'.

This is what Eckhart Tolle means, according to my understanding. *The Power of Now* is indeed a life-changing book.

———————

If you are living in a society that has been created and governed by laws, then automatically, the judgement of someone takes place because of the law of the land, and maybe for someone's doing, he/she is sent to jail. But in reality, that judgement is not correct, as it is not his 'doing'. Is my understanding correct?

Yes. But, of course, he has to bear the consequences of his actions as per the legal provisions, as per the laws framed to govern society. Otherwise, we would have a lawless land.

While on the subject of 'judgement', let's keep that aside for a moment and talk about the judgements we make on others. A spiritual seeker on the path will start investigating what his judgement is based on. That is the journey of seeking. And one will inevitably come to the conclusion that most of our judgements are based on what we think the other 'did', or what we 'did'. Nobody is the doer of their actions; the 'Lord' is the 'Sole Doer'. Why do all masters say, 'Do not criticize others?' Because, as Maharaj says, 'Everything is the affair of the Brahman, so to criticize someone is to criticize Brahman.'

With the understanding, the dialogue that used to take place—that of criticism and malice and hatred towards others or oneself—vanishes. You might not like a certain person who may be close to you for being who they are, but the finger-pointing has gone. The sting of 'doership' has been removed. You may still have preferences, because we all have preferences, but that dialogue in your mind of 'this person should not be that way, he must change or she must change,' is gone. You may find that you are gravitating towards a new set of friends; be happy with that. It is a natural process. But there is no animosity anymore or negativity towards the others that you are gravitating away from.

What about all the desires I have? Shall I endeavour to get them fulfilled, or shall I just sit back and wait for them to be fulfilled by God?

Sure, go ahead and try to get them fulfilled, knowing that whether they are fulfilled or not is God's Will. Desire arises. It is the ego that claims ownership of the desire, and then gets frustrated if the desire is not fulfilled.

Is it the desire of God, then?

Desire is desire. When we say 'God's desire', we are looking at God as an individual, because we are thinking in terms of being an individual. God, the Source, is all there is. We all have desires. The sage does not say, 'I have no desires', because the sage knows that the arising of a desire is natural. But to be entangled in the desire and claim ownership of the desire—the sage does not do that. Nor does the sage pursue the desire to the detriment of himself and others.

My teacher gave this simple example to illustrate the difference between a desire arising in the mind of a sage and that of an ordinary person: It is a Sunday afternoon and the thought comes, 'Let's have a beer'. An ordinary person gets up from the sofa, opens the fridge but does not see the beer. There is none left. He yells at his wife, asking why she did not remember to keep some beer in the fridge. He then goes down to the shop but, it being a Sunday, the shop is closed. This leads to frustration. He gets so involved in his desire that he creates much misery for himself, he blames the wife for being careless, the shop for it being closed, and so on. What was a natural desire for beer has now been extended in the duration of time, with frustration being the outcome, and suffering has been created for himself and others.

In the sage, the desire arises, he opens the fridge, sees that there is no beer and says, 'Oh, there is no beer in the fridge.' For the sage it ends there. He doesn't blame anyone, he doesn't create drama around it. Of course, he may ask his wife, or even express annoyance, but there is no further involvement as he does not blame her. He may go down to the shop, but when he sees that the shop is closed, he understands that it was not his destiny for the desire to be fulfilled. So be it. That is the only difference between a sage and the ordinary person. What we do is pursue our desire to the detriment of our relationship with others or with ourselves. The sage does not do that. So if you can live your life like that, the drama in life is finished.

Someone mentioned to me that one particular sentence from one of Ramesh Balsekar's books impacted him deeply. It was— 'Act as if you are dead and then do whatever you like.' What does it mean? It refers to the ego. Our fear of death is the fear of the death of the ego; the ego does not want to die. We have no problem with deep sleep and in fact, we look forward to it, but the ego dies in deep sleep. In the waking state the ego has the problem—it does not want to die. Of course, the ego is needed as the operational element in daily living. So obviously, death of the ego refers to the death of the sense of 'doership'. When the sense of 'doership' dies, you are free.

———

If everything is about God's Will, then are our actions and reactions also God's Will?
Yes.

Then what should we do?
You should do exactly that which you think and feel you should do, knowing that it is God, the Source, operating through this body-mind instrument.

But then, everyone will do wrong things and say it's God's Will.
This is the classic argument of the ego. It all depends on one's nature. If someone puts a gun in your hands and says, 'Shoot!' you will not do it if it is not in your nature. What's more, this teaching does not absolve you of your responsibility to society. The repercussions of your actions are also God's Will.

———

If it is all about being rather than doing, then why is it necessary to do anything?

It is not about it being necessary to do anything. It is about doing that which you are meant to do. It is like asking, 'Why is it necessary to go to the bathroom?' Can you even control the fact? It is precisely what Arjuna said to Lord Krishna, 'Why should I fight my preceptors?' And he put his bow and arrow down. And Krishna replied, 'Your genetics are of a warrior, your conditioning has been that of a warrior, you have been trained to fight, so pick up that bow and fight! Because, it is not "you" doing that act, as Time I have already killed them.'

So surely if you have been designed a certain way, to do certain things, you have to honour that. You see, it is a very tricky thing. The ego comes in through the back door by asking a question like this. If your nature is not one to sit back and relax, your attempt at trying to sit back and relax is in fact 'doership'.

I have been enjoying your talks including the references to Ramesh Balsekar and his teaching. When you ask us not to do this or that, for example, whether to react to a thought arising or let thoughts pass through, are you not influencing what God is directing us to do? I am 83 years of age. I started reading Jiddu Krishnamurti more than half a century ago.

There is no question of 'me' influencing what God is directing us to do, as I have no power as a separate 'individual entity' to do so.

Nobody does. It seems you have perhaps inadvertently set me up separate from 'God', whereas the teaching that flows through 'me' is coming from the same Source, call it 'God' or 'Consciousness'. We are 'All' instruments through whom God's Will functions.

The whole point is that what you hear through these talks (or any talks you come across) is fresh conditioning, that may or may not alter the existing conditioning (sometimes, it can transform it overnight).

Now, whether or not the teaching has any impact on you is determined by the 'will' of the Source; it is clearly not in your control, nor is it in mine, more so because you have been given the conditioning of 50 years of reading J. Krishnamurti. And by 'impact' I mean the peace of mind it has brought to your daily living. This has not been addressed in your question. For, what is the value in 'enjoying the talks' if they do not deliver this peace?

———————

I have been trying to be in the moment. Sometimes, I feel that the thought is automatically embraced, and such thought is usually negative. Can you please help with how to sustain the practice of being in the moment and are there any ways to bring the awareness back when the mind becomes stronger?

By 'embraced' I take it that you mean that involvement in the thought happens. Involvement generally happens when there is a sense of 'doership' (myself or the other) associated with the thought. Sometimes the very effort being made to be in the moment takes one further away from the moment. Rather, witnessing what happens would bring about a shift in perspective over the course of time.

It is the understanding that stops the involvement in horizontal thinking. I do not encourage practices as such, as it is simply the 'seeing' and the 'understanding' that gradually cuts off the involvement in thinking. As Nisargadatta Maharaj would say, 'All one needs to do is to "abide in one's beingness".'

How does one make residing in the moment one's natural state of being? Does there come a point where you are no longer bringing your awareness back to the moment as you are just residing in the moment?

It can only 'happen'. As the understanding sinks deeper and deeper, one notices that one is less involved in thinking than one used to be. Allow it to 'happen' rather than keep 'doing' something so it happens faster.

Residing in the moment already is one's natural state of being, it is only the thinking mind that takes one away from it, so to speak. Therefore, the absence of the compulsive thinking undertaken by the thinking mind, makes one rest in being. As the understanding sinks deeper and deeper, one notices that one is less involved in thinking than one used to be.

I simply wanted to thank you for always being there. I have recently gone through an episode of paralysing depression (family problems), and it wasn't until I finally 'remembered' again, that I have been able to come to my senses.

My spiritual life has a life of its own. It's like a self-maintaining garden, even when I am crushed under a load of depression and unable to tend that garden consciously. Amazing how that happens!

When you say, 'It wasn't until I finally remembered', what actually happened is that 'It remembered you'. Such is the Grace of the Source.

Nisargadatta Maharaj used to say—to people who visited him in his attic and didn't resonate with what he said—that the process had already begun. By their coming there, the seed had already been planted and would sprout sooner or later. My teacher Rameshji would say, 'Your head is already in the tiger's mouth.' I think he borrowed that from Ramana Maharshi.

Wishing you much strength in dealing with the family problems. Family bonds are the strongest karmic bonds. As it is said, 'We can't choose our family like we can choose our friends.' Though, we really can't choose our friends either. Or our enemies, for that matter!

I was seriously ill with muscular dystrophy. I have been studying the Buddha's teachings as well as Sri Nisargadatta Maharaj's for several years, without a Guru. For the last six months I have been reciting

mantras and singing bhajans, but despite that I'm afraid of emptiness
… that fear and depression. I ask for your personal edification.

I am sorry to hear about your illness. You are not alone; most of humanity is afraid of 'emptiness, fear and depression'. In your case it has taken an illness to bring you to this despair, but you will be surprised at how many healthy people also suffer from these conditions that plague the mind. Genetics and conditioning do play a large part in this.

No one knows what the next moment brings; sometimes pleasure and sometimes pain. While we have a preference for pleasures inbuilt in us, the running away from pain is what stops with the understanding. It is accepted (and we don't have to like it) as a part of the movement of daily living.

While there are various options to consider including psychotherapy, nothing can really be 'done' about it as a 'spiritual' remedy, except the witnessing of it. The seeing is the only doing necessary. That is why Maharaj used to point people towards simply 'abiding in their being'.

It is interesting to note that at the centre of these feelings is the 'me', identified with name and form as a separate entity. The 'me' is afraid of emptiness. 'I don't know who I am, if I am empty.' The 'me' is fearful. 'What will happen to me?' The stronger the identification, the stronger the feeling of separation. And these feelings get intensified by the deep-rooted sense of 'doership', of something I did or did not do, or what someone else did or did not do to 'me'.

Almost everyone's story is one of suffering in some form or the other, and fear. After all, the Buddha said, 'Samsara is dukkha. Nirvana is shanti.' And most of our thoughts are fear-based thoughts. As the Buddhists say, 'Most if not all fears come from the fear of death.' And while it 'appears' we are afraid of our physical death, it is the 'me' that is afraid of its absence, of its death, as it were.

The fact that, as you mentioned, you are studying the Buddha's teachings, as well as Maharaj's, and chanting mantras and singing bhajans, means that you have been showered with Grace, without which even this much would not have happened. So do consider your glass half full and not half empty.

Thank you for such a warm response and sympathy. I just finished reading and studying your wonderful book 'Pointers from Ramesh Balsekar'. The book made a strong impression on me. I know all I want is Peace, not enlightenment and security. This 'Great Peace' is the Source (Nothing). Knowing this, I'm less afraid of death and don't feel sorry for myself. This is my discovery. Your book is the quintessence of the teachings of Sri Nisargadatta Maharaj and Sri Ramesh Balsekar. Thank you very much for your hard work, compassion and support. Take a bow.

You are most welcome. You were meant to come across the teaching. You did not find the teaching but the teaching found you. I am just like a postman delivering a letter that contains an important message that is being carried down through the ages. It is what one reads in the letter that impacts one. Of course, gratitude to the postman who is the instrument through whom the letter is delivered arises. At the end of it all, thanking me is like your left hand thanking your right hand.

―――――――

I have been reading texts on Advaita for quite some time now. While I continue on my spiritual path, there are still a few questions in my mind. It would be helpful to receive your thoughts on these:

I work with entrepreneurs and really admire what they do. I was listening to an entrepreneur while he said, 'Whenever I see a big problem in society, I can't stop myself from solving it.' A thought arose in my mind, 'Is there really a problem?' According to the spiritual teachings I have received, there is no problem and the world is the way it is meant to be.

For the entrepreneur you mentioned, there is a problem. For you there isn't. Each one has their own understanding based on their nature (genetics and conditioning) and their resultant world view.

Then the next moment I was thinking, are my spiritual teachings leading me to inaction? If so, how will I make progress in this world as I will never act on anything, and simply observe. Can you help me resolve this confusion?

Certainly, to make progress in the material world one needs to act, one needs to engage the 'working mind'. If it is one's nature to act, then one must honour it and act. Using the teaching to 'not act' is also a subtle form of 'doership', employed by the ego. On the other hand, if you have adequate material resources and don't have the need to work, then you may choose not to work if that (work) is not in your nature to do. Deep down, you know the answer to this question.

Another question is related to suffering. Recently there was an accident in Surat where more than 20 kids lost their lives. Was this meant to be? What justifies such painful deaths?

Yes, the understanding is that it was meant to be else it would not have happened. Nothing really justifies painful deaths, just as nothing justifies the birth of handicapped children. What harm have they done, and to whom? In this world, there is a lot that doesn't make sense. But that is the nature of things as they are. It is we who seek meaning in a world of duality—where extreme polarities exist, the good and bad, rich and poor, and so on. The puny human intellect cannot understand the basis of God's Will.

Does a sage transcend this pain?

The sage experiences 'pain in the moment' completely, without building a story around it and asking 'Why?' questions, which the ordinary person does. Grief will arise in the moment, but it will not get extended in the duration of time, into mourning.

I have often heard the word 'Choicelessness' being mentioned by people who are on the spiritual path. What exactly is choicelessness?

By 'Choicelessness', it is meant that one's choice itself is 'choiceless'. This is because what you think is your choice, is truly not 'your' choice. Your choice is based on your genes and conditioning—two factors over which you had no control. Choicelessness does not mean that you don't choose—let's say, blue or green. It means that you choose what is in your nature to choose.

'Choice' means you have the ability to make and take a decision. I have to decide whether to take a left or a right turn on the road—that is my free will and my choice. The average person thinks that it is 'my will' which is making me take the left or right turn. But, in reality, there are a lot of factors that determine your decision, and these factors are not in your control.

You all may feel that it is your will that made you come here, but the fact is that if I had not written a book, and if Khushru (the organiser) had not read it, I would not have been invited for this talk. Further, if I were not a publisher—my book probably wouldn't have got published. *(Laughter)*

If that stream of events had not happened, I would not be here with you today.

Similarly, how much of 'your will' did you exercise to come here? It's possible that you may not have been on the mailing list and, therefore, not seen the announcement of the talk. You could have got stuck in traffic, or another engagement could have come up. So do you see the chain of events, which goes far back, that influences what you decide to do at some later date? Yet you feel it's one action of 'mine' that is 'my choice'.

Day-to-day living requires one to make and take decisions. One has to because that is how we, as human beings, function— by taking decisions. All I am saying is that you must remember that the outcome of your decision is not in your control, because the outcome will be according to God's Will. What's more, don't indulge in 'what-ifs' and blame yourself, thus—'If I had not done that, then this wouldn't have happened,' and so on. Don't blame yourself because what you thought was your free will was truly not your free will.

Can you illustrate this by some example, if possible?
In the Bhagavad Gita, Arjuna saw the enemy's entire army positioned against him, whereas on his part, he had chosen only Lord Krishna. So he told Krishna, 'I can fight my relatives, but I cannot fight my preceptors,' and having said that, he put his bow and quiver of arrows down. Krishna said, 'Look here, you were born in the warrior caste, your whole training in life has been to be a warrior, you are designed to fight ... so you pick up that bow and fight because that is your dharma. And please don't think you are killing them, because I—as Time—have already killed them.'

One day at my guru Rameshji's home, a man of around 65 years of age came for the talks. He had been a veteran soldier somewhere in Europe. He said that for every night since the end of the war, he had broken down in tears because he had killed some soldiers of the enemy. And Rameshji told him the same thing. He said, 'Look, you belong to a family of soldiers (the man had said that even his grandfather was a soldier), you were conscripted into the military when you were a young boy, your conditioning was to fight for the country, so why are you taking ownership of the fact that you killed the enemy? If you realise that you were meant to kill, then you will be at peace.' And this man just started sobbing. He said, 'I am now ready to die tomorrow.' So, let's not become attached to what we think is our choice and free will. Not being attached is a liberating feeling.

Hitler was born because it was God's Will, and so was Osama Bin Laden. By 'God' I mean the Source or Consciousness, and not an individual sitting up there in heaven. If God did not create 'bad' people, then who created them? There cannot be two 'Sources', otherwise it would beget the question that where did they come from? The Source created Hitler, and the Source created Mother Teresa. This is what Rameshji used to say.

Consciousness does not differentiate. One of the more painful facets of humanity is that of handicapped children and you wonder how God could do that. God would probably answer that by saying, 'Nobody asks Me why I created healthy children!' We don't know the basis of God's Will. The Nirbhaya case (someone in the audience had raised the issue of a recent gang rape that had created a mass revolution of sorts in India) is horrific. But what it does to each of us, how each of us is impacted individually, how we are impacted collectively as a group, what it makes us feel—in other words, what role that event was supposed to play, will be played according to God's Will.

When Jesus said while he was nailed to the cross: 'Not my will Oh Lord, but Thine, be done,' it signified his total surrender to God's Will.

Now, as far as the perpetrators of the Nirbhaya rape were concerned, thankfully they were all nabbed and the law of the land will take its own course. What punishment the Court metes out to them would ultimately be God's Will. Just as it was God's Will that they be nabbed. A happening may be God's Will, but it does not absolve the individual of the consequences of his action and his responsibility to society—which is also God's Will.

This kind of approach can be perceived as fatalistic, and it can border on inaction.

Do exactly what you think and feel you should do, but know that the results of your action are not in your control. This does not mean that you 'sit back'. It's not in your nature to sit back. Fatalism is felt by the ego—it feels helpless with this approach. It does not like it. But it's not that. Deep down, the arrow has hit home. With this approach, you will be more relaxed when you do things. You will not be that attached. You will still do them but there will be a lightness because you know that, in any case, the results are not in your control. It will not make you fatalistic; you will, in fact, enjoy doing those things much more than you did before. Why? Because it will no longer be 'you' doing them. You have the realisation that it is happening through you.

As the famous Russian ballet dancer Nidjinsky once said: 'Nidjinsky dances best when Nidjinsky is not there.'

Could Advaita be perceived as the lazy man's guide to life and living?
A 27-year-young man, who was impacted by the teaching, once
said to me, 'I am not in "thinking mind" mode; I play video games
all the time so I am in "working mind" mode.' What he meant to
say was that he was not sitting idle but keeping his mind engaged.
Then he went on to say, 'It's my destiny to play video games and
not to work,' and so on.

See, the ego is very naughty. It plays these games of deception.
At the heart of the matter is the burning question: 'Who am I
without "my" mind?' The ego is afraid that it would lose its
identity, its sense of self, if the mind was not kept engaged in some
activity or another.

The beauty is to see that it was made that way. Sometimes,
the mind is made to be conniving, but the realisation is that a
person is not a conniving 'being'. How can a human being be
conniving? A 'being' can simply 'be'—being. So, if you start
looking at people from that perspective, you will be more relaxed.

This does not mean one should not tell someone—let's say
your son—to stop playing video games throughout the day, if
that's what arises. You should not prevent what comes naturally
to you as well. But deep down you know that you're not targeting
an individual 'me' but a person programmed by his genes and
conditioning—both factors that are beyond his control. When
this happens, it removes the conflict and disharmony from
relationships.

But, what do I do when my son uses that same argument with me when confronted?

He has not been exposed to the teaching, you have! Anyway, the point is that you now realise that he is playing out a script based on his destiny. He is meant to think the way he is thinking and do what he is doing, and you are meant to be there to put forward your point of view. But his problem is that you keep repeating your point of view.

See, the ego never likes to be told the same thing over and over again. He will rebel against that. All you need to do is plant the seed, and then let go of constantly trying to put someone on a particular path. It's just like constantly watering the seed which would destroy it, instead of giving it the time and environment to sprout and grow. You know, as I have said before, our mother never once said 'No' to us. And because of that, all of us siblings grew up quite well-disciplined. So, the next time when you see that that's the way the person's mind is working, you will perhaps give a quiet smile of understanding.

Another thing is that he wants to come closer but there's something holding him back. I know it's a matter of time, it will happen when it's supposed to happen, but if one wants to hasten that process, what does one do?

Doing something about that would mean a lot of 'doership' on your part. He wants to come closer to you because of who you are. So, by going out of your way to do something in order to make your son come closer, you are, in a sense, going away from your own centre. It will be the destiny of that person who is attracted to you, to come to you. And his journey lies in that journey towards you. I would say you have to be exactly as you are. So, if the ego steps in and wants to hasten things, that would create a disturbance in the dynamic—of course, if that happened, then even that would be destined. There is something in you that is wanting the other person to come to you; just remain a witness to that. Investigate those moments—what is your state which is drawing him to you? Be present for him as 'that'.

The best thing that you can do is to just witness. However, the point is that witnessing is not something you can 'do'. Witnessing happens when the sense of 'doership' is not there. 'Witnessing' is not the same as 'observing' because when we observe, we judge. Observing is the 'me' observing something done by the individual. When you are impartial and have not established a point of view, it is then that witnessing happens. The ego cannot try to witness because the ego, as the thinking mind, is not the witness. Witnessing is the total collapse of the thinking mind, which is the characteristic of the ego, into the total acceptance of this present moment.

So does this mean that the whole game is that the ego wants to survive with its story, its attachment to certain feelings and pleasures, and the witness has to watch this game?

The witness is that which is aware of this happening. So when the awareness arises that 'I am in a game', that is the witness. The more the awareness that you are in a game—the leela, the more the witnessing is happening.

Sometimes the game gets very intense and one forgets …

That's the flip-flop. But with time that starts reducing. It's like climbing a hundred steps … one step at a time. Life is a learning curve. With this understanding, your involvement in situations starts reducing. Your drama is playing out in consciousness. If you were not conscious, there would be no drama being played out. So, the teaching is just pointing you back to the consciousness, which is the witness. You can't have a problem with someone if you are not conscious. In deep sleep, you cannot have a problem with anyone.

———————

I have a friend who has bad habits of drinking, smoking, and using abusive language. He has been like this since the age of 15! My question is, 'Is this all done by God? How can God make him addicted to these things?' Could you please suggest some prayer or remedy so that he can leave all these bad habits. Please suggest some path which I can perform but without his knowledge.

All 'good' and 'bad' habits depend primarily on our upbringing, especially during our formative years. And our upbringing depends on the conditioning we received—how our parents treated us, the school we went to, the economic strata we were born into, our geographical location, our religion and beliefs, our relationship with friends and colleagues, and so on. None of this is in our control. In addition to this is the genetic blueprint we carry, which is also not in our control, so to speak.

It seems that you perhaps conceive God as an individual, like us, and then wonder how He could make your friend imbibe those bad habits. God is the Source, the 'Totality' of 'What Is', whereas we are asking the question from our own limited perspective as individuals with a sense of 'doership'.

So we ask, 'How can God "do" this?' Just like we ask, 'How can God create handicapped children? What harm have they done?' But no one asks, 'Why did God create healthy children?' Similarly, you are questioning why God created these bad habits in your friend, but what about the good habits in another friend? We do not accept this basic duality of life and so we suffer.

It might be worthwhile for you to refer your friend to a good therapist, if his behaviour is troubling you. Prayers and remedies are not the only solution for addictions and deep-rooted negative behaviour patterns. Also, we need to keep in mind that people are not addicted to the actual act of smoking and drinking as such, but rather the feeling it evokes in them (which they want more of).

When an alcoholic disciple asked Sathya Sai Baba to help him get rid of his alcoholism, Sathya Sai Baba mentioned, 'Next time you have a drink, dedicate it to Me.' And the disciple followed his instructions and eventually left alcohol. Simply because, over time he could not get himself to have a drink when he thought of his Guru.

I found your interpretation of free will to be fascinating. This idea that we don't actually have free will because our genes and conditioning impact our thoughts/choices is an interesting notion.

But this got me thinking that perhaps our genes and conditioning can be viewed as a result of our free will since it is our past karma that dictated our genetic makeup and mental conditioning in this lifetime. From my understanding of Advaita Vedanta, we 'chose' this experience. Every moment is a return on a past intention; a karmic debt playing out in each birth. We are the 'Creator' of our experience.

Am I accurate in my understanding that it is all indeed our free will? That perhaps what appears to be 'uncontrollable variables' (like genes and societal conditioning) are actually variables that were chosen by us, which perhaps means that our current experience is a culmination of free will choices?

I have deep reverence for the teachings of Sri Nisargadatta Maharaj and Sri Ramana Maharshi. Their enlightening forms have played an impactful role on my spiritual evolution in this lifetime, as has the Bhagavad Gita. Thank you for being a wonderful messenger of these Divine teachings.

I am glad the teaching has found its way to your heart.

If we follow through on your concept, it would then beget the question: What was the basis of free will in the first birth? Who determined the genetics and conditioning then? Therefore, in that sense, it is not 'our' past karma but rather 'the' past karma (Prarabdh karma) that plays out, and brings about what is meant to 'happen'. Karma—referring to not 'my' action but rather the fundamental 'cause-effect', 'action-consequence' loop.

More importantly, what you have outlined on free will is a concept, much like what you have heard through the videos and as part of the teaching regarding free will, which is another concept. Both are not the Truth; they only point the way. The main point to note is—which one delivers peace of mind to you in daily living? Else, what use are either of these concepts? This is perhaps something worthy of contemplation or reflection.

However, and I might be wrong, my guess is that if you are drawn to the teachings of Sri Ramana Maharshi and Sri Nisargadatta Maharaj, you know the answer to this already.

You and Ramesh have helped me to see that who I am as the individual self is based on my design (genes and conditioning). However, one might criticize the teaching for being too focused on the individual self. Nisargadatta Maharaj said, 'Realisation is of the fact that you are not a person ... Personal entity and enlightenment cannot go together.' How would you respond to this?

You have raised a question that comes up often, for those familiar with Maharaj's and Rameshji's teaching.

Maharaj was not concerned with the 'person' he was speaking to, and he would say that he was directly implanting the seed in the consciousness. Rameshji, being one of the translators, realised that this caused some confusion in some seekers. After all, they were asking questions from their individual point of view. Therefore, in his teaching, Rameshji decided to directly address the individual, the ego, and take it through the process of uprooting the sense of 'doership' (not the ego itself).

In one of his talks, Rameshji said something to the effect of, 'Maharaj's book was titled *I Am That*. For me it's rather, "*That is you, me, he and she.*"' Therefore, these were two different approaches to the same destination—peace of mind. Maharaj referred to this as 'abiding in one's being', 'the conscious presence' and so on, while Rameshji showed the way through the annihilation of the sense of 'doership', and therefore, all the cartwheels and shenanigans of the thinking mind, which brings about a natural 'witnessing' or 'abiding' in one's being.

When Maharaj told Rameshji that when he taught he would not parrot Maharaj's words, this is perhaps how it happened—through the teaching presenting itself in a different style.

And, of course, personal entity and enlightenment cannot go together, simply because a person cannot 'do' anything to get enlightened. The absence of the sense of 'doership' is the enlightenment.

———————

I only desire 'Brahma Gyan', but this body is ailing with pain and keeps my mind occupied in the pain. I tried many types of treatments but failed to be cured. What is your opinion about physical pain and an unhealthy body, and how do I not get occupied with it and stay focused on the 'Brahma Tattva' at all times? What am I to do or not do?

Sorry to hear about your pain. Acceptance of the pain, and the fact that pain is there because it is God's Will, brings one a certain peace. We normally tend to extend purely physical pain into mental suffering by building a story around it (as 'my pain', 'Why did this happen to me?' and so on). With the understanding, it is the thinking mind that is annihilated (comprising all thoughts of blame, shame, guilt, and so on; in other words— the story of 'me and my pain'). This way, one is living in the moment, and honouring whatever arises in the moment. That's why Maharaj said, 'The road is the goal.' Leave it to Grace to decide whether or not to fulfil your desire for 'Brahma Gyan'.

On another note (as we are discussing the subject of 'pain'), when my spiritual teacher's migraine of 30 years disappeared one morning, he said that he then understood that 'absence of pain is the greatest pleasure'.

So, given the situation you are in, all you can do is try, when the pain is not overbearing.

ANGER

'The anger in the moment is not the
problem. It is the involvement in
the anger that is the real problem.'

If you think that you will be calm in a particular situation but when that situation arises, you react differently, then do you say to yourself that it is God's Will as you did not mean to react that way, and not feel guilty about it?

Yes, you have answered your own question quite well. You may feel regret about your reaction, and may even apologize if someone got hurt, but no guilt or shame, as there is the total understanding that it was not in your control. And you don't really say this to yourself, rather, it is the understanding that arises that whatever happened in that moment was precisely what was supposed to happen. If at all there is any involvement in the reaction, for example, 'I should not have reacted that way,' then the involvement is cut off by the understanding and one is no longer involved. Of course, when it is cut off, is God's Will.

———

In the last few days there has been some news about the death of a child and a march organised for it, by the public. How do you see the teaching in this context?

What happened is horrific, there is no question about it. Would anger arise? Of course it would. Nothing changes. But you know that there is a Divine force which has orchestrated all of this. Yet, you will do precisely what you feel you should.

So, if you feel like organising a march, you will. But you have the acceptance of the fact that it happened because it is the will of God. Why is this the will of God? We would never know. We can never know the will of God.

I have lived in an ashram for six years and now I realise that it has been futile. I have come back to Mumbai. Someone called from the ashram and I lost my cool with them. I know that it is the same electricity which flows through everyone, but when the situation arises, I forget it. How do you make this teaching a part of your life?
You come across a teaching when you are meant to. That intelligence, that part of the Divine nature, has to be trusted to do its job.

Now there are so many factors that result in anger arising. The anger in the moment is not the problem. It is the involvement in the anger that is the real problem. That is where the teaching comes in. But then, the guilt arises about getting angry. That is where the teaching comes in again, because the understanding is that if it were in my control I would not have got angry. It actually proves that it is not in my control.

What happens is that witnessing starts happening more and more—witnessing of patterns, witnessing of reactions, in this case, anger. Earlier it was blind anger, reactivity, engagement and conflict. Now the realisation is there. This teaching is like a torch, the light of which falls on something which was not looked at earlier. So it is the understanding that starts operating, not the 'you' who is going to sort this mess out about 'Why do I get angry?' It is seen in a neutral light without judgement. Anger may still arise, but you will not resent the other person like you did earlier. You will not resent yourself like you do now. You are not judging yourself, like 'I should not be this way,' or 'I should be this way'. The 'should' starts dropping away. And witnessing is what starts changing the dynamic, because you no longer hold on to what the other did or what you did that made you angry. That starts transforming relationships.

CONTROL

'If your own breath, which is the foundation of your existence, is not in your control, then what degree of control do you have in your life?'

How does one cope with the uncertainty of life? What can one do to fortify oneself against it?

The fact is that the bedrock of life is uncertainty, because we never know what the next moment is going to bring—sometimes pain, sometimes pleasure. In the initial stages, the 'me' wants to hold on to only pleasure. 'I only want things which are pleasurable to me, to happen. I do not want pain.' Quite right, but life keeps teaching one repeatedly that that is not what life is about, for life is duality, sometimes pleasure and sometimes pain. Without this acceptance, what was an initial level of suffering, which is the pain in the moment, gets compounded by my not wanting that pain. Therefore, the only way to cope with uncertainty is to accept that uncertainty is the fundamental design of life.

The 'me' can keep running after pleasures till it reaches a point of exhaustion, which is when it realises that these pleasures are not delivering true happiness. Why? Because they come and go, and so the happiness does not last. It then reaches the understanding that nobody guarantees pleasures all the time, in life.

If the investigation is taken further, then what happens is that the perspective shifts. Questions arise, such as: Who is it that wants only pleasure and not pain? Who is it that wants to fortify himself/herself against the uncertainty of life? Who feels the uncertainty of life? It is the 'me', with its sense of control. The 'me' realises, 'I am not able to control my life to have only pleasures.' And with that understanding, the controlling aspect of the 'me' starts dissolving. As Jesus said, 'Not my will Oh Lord, but Thine, be done.' That starts becoming the perspective on one's own life. Then, the acceptance is that I do not have control over what the next moment brings. I am not able to micromanage my life to safeguard against things that might be painful to me. So the hold of the 'me' starts loosening up.

There is a tremendous gift in accepting that there is a lot in your life which is beyond your control. Your next thought is not in your control. Your next breath is not in your control. When you fall asleep is not in your control. Gradually, you start accepting life, more and more. Your thinking mind starts getting disengaged. The light of being, of awareness, starts shining through and you live your life in peace, in harmony with the will of the 'Lord'.

So the way to fortify oneself against uncertainty is to be open to it. As Nisargadatta Maharaj said, 'The expected seldom happens whereas the unexpected always does!'

––––––––––

I have this need to improve myself. What shall I do?
If you feel motivated to do something to improve yourself, go ahead. It must be honoured, because the feeling has come from

within. Do precisely that which you think and feel you should do. But the frustration happens when we feel that we can control the outcome of that effort. That is why the Gita says that the fruits of your actions are not yours.

I will read you something which actually answers your question, which I read out at a talk the other day. 'The truth is that life is an ever-going process, ever-renewing, and it is just meant to be lived but not lived for. It is something that cannot be squeezed into a self-constructed security pattern, a game of rigid control and clever manipulation. Instead, to be what I term a quality human being, one has to be transparently real and have the courage to be what he is.' This is by the martial arts expert, Bruce Lee.

It is courage to be what you are. It takes courage to know that nobody truly does anything.

———————

Do I need to make any effort or will this acceptance of having no control happen automatically?
It is automatic. You just have to look at your own life. Spend 15 minutes in the evening and review the events of the day— that is all the effort you need to make. You will come to this conclusion yourself. My teacher would say, 'Look at the events of the day and you will realise that you either saw something, smelled something, tasted something, touched something or heard something in the course of the day, on the basis of which you took an action. Now, did you have any control over all

that you saw, tasted, touched, smelled, or heard? Then how can you call it your action? You had no control over all the factors that made you take a decision, yet you call it your decision. For example, you happened to be at a certain place at a certain time, when you saw something. Did you choose that? And on the basis of what you saw, you performed an action or took a decision.'

The gift of the teaching is to see life in its entirety and oneness, to see that it is all interconnected. To see the glory of how the universe structures each moment in your life to be precisely the way it is, is true humility. If you are having a bad day at work, the universe has conspired to give you that bad day at work, if you will. It is a relief because you know 'you' did not do it. But we feel it is all in our control.

We feel our emotions should not be the way they are, but there are so many planetary, energetic influences over which you have no control. Who says it is your emotion? Look at the effect the moon has on the tides. And, 70% of the human body is water, so you can imagine the effect it has on us. Who has decided the chemical composition of the fluids in your body, on a particular day? Who has decided what has transpired in the course of the day? You were crossing the road and you saw something that upset you. Did you plan that? Can you see the number of factors that are contributing to each and every moment you are living and breathing on this planet? It is a Divine conspiracy.

———————

If everything is God's Will, how does one react to different situations in life? How does one deal with others? Do I just say, 'It is God's Will, what can I do?' and accept everything and everyone, and get along?

You should do exactly what you think and feel you should do, knowing deep down that neither are you the doer, nor is anyone else. And, deep down you have the total acceptance that the outcome is not in your control. All you can do is do your best.

You deal with others with the understanding that everyone is an instrument of the Divine, and they have been shaped by the Divine. Just like you have been.

You will not lose your discretion. You have to continue to take decisions, because that is the mechanism of daily living, but you will no longer blame yourself if the outcome is not as you had intended. There is a total acceptance of what is happening, including your pain and suffering. Most of us are avoiding the pain, but if you accept it and face the pain, you will be quite surprised at the peace the acceptance brings. After all, it is one's experience that life is pleasure one moment, pain another.

———————

If one is to acknowledge that nothing is under one's control, does that mean that we coexist passively without trying to influence anything and accept things the way they are? Or does it mean that you still react in a manner such that you believe is right, but without necessarily getting too engaged in the outcome? I face certain situations at the office, so could you give an example related to the workplace?

Absolutely. Let's say you are at a senior level in your office, and have many people reporting to you. One of them is someone who loves working hard. You are happy with his or her performance. Now, let's say you have a team member who is not working as hard as you would like him to. You keep asking him to improve his performance, but he is still not performing. At some point, you will understand that this man is working to the best of his ability; there is no point pushing him beyond that. You have the acceptance that each individual is shaped the way they are; they have the skill sets that they have been given, and they may have reached their limits in terms of performance.

Therefore, all you can do is try up to a point, to help him perform better, and then you let go. You decide whether or not he is productive to the organisation. It doesn't mean you have to coexist passively, without trying to influence anything. Yet, you do not hold people personally responsible for not being the way you would want them to be; for not meeting your standards. So you do not judge and criticize him for his performance, in that sense. Of course, what you do is to evaluate his performance in relation to the expectations from the job, and then take a decision.

What we do is point fingers and blame people. In this case, we blame the staff member for not doing his best, for not meeting 'our' version of what is best. We do not see things objectively. We are very good at judging and criticizing others as well as ourselves.

DEATH

'Everyone's journey is a journey of loss.
To lose, in order to find who you truly are.
To lose, to find that which cannot be lost.'

What do I tell my child who asks me what death is? I do not want to introduce the concept of death to her, I do not want her to fear it, and at the same time I want to explain it to her. How do I do it? I always postpone this discussion. I go blank and I say, 'I will tell you tomorrow.'

I remember the story of the Buddha, whose father kept him confined to the palace, to prevent him from seeing decay, disease and death. He wanted to prevent his son from becoming a mystic, as it was predicted that the Buddha would become either a great emperor or a great spiritual master. And that action is precisely what went against the father's plan. Since he was walled up inside a palace that had only pleasures and no pain, the young Siddhartha Gautama wondered what was outside the palace walls and when he rode out, he was shocked at what he saw.

So firstly, children do not have the fear of death. It is we who condition their minds with our fear of death. The child emerges from 'beingness'. The first two or three years of being is pure being for the child. Everything is magical to the child. The child has no notion that he/she is going to die. Many children at the age of six or seven, start asking questions about death. This is because, they get introduced to the concept through their environment. For example, they see something on TV, they see a pet die, a friend mentions the word 'death', and so on.

Now, you must tell the child whatever you think and feel you should, because the child is growing under the umbrella or protective influence of his/her parents. You know your child best. You don't need to ask ten people what you should tell your child. You just have to say what is appropriate, with awareness, because why would that be wrong? To postpone the enquiry may not be the right course of action, as the child will start wondering why he/she is not getting the answers. Yes, you might wonder about what kind of examples to give the child, to make him/her understand the concept of death. You could, for example, make reference to how the seasons change from spring to summer, autumn and winter. You would know best what examples your child would relate to.

So there should not be any fear of the right or wrong way of answering this question—which, in turn, leads to not answering the question. Postponing the answer can create frustration and confusion in the child. There is never a right or wrong answer. If you accept yourself the way God has made you, your views will be equally valid. So there may be a concern whether one is answering it the right way, but to postpone it because of this is to postpone a situation unnecessarily.

On the other hand, it is quite beautiful that such questions are being asked by the child. That is actually pure intelligence operating, discovering, wondering. That must be honoured rather than saying, 'Don't ask me this, don't bother me now.' The child must not be made to feel that it is not right to ask about these things.

Everyone's journey is the journey of 'me'. We are born into the 'me'—'me and my story'. That is why we take birth. The child's journey will unravel like everyone else's, like it is meant to. The journey of life is actually the journey of the death of 'me' with its sense of 'doership'; the death of the 'me and my story'. In duality, death is the opposite of birth. Death is not the opposite of life. Life is what is lived between these two points.

———————

My son died in a car accident along with two other boys. The thought keeps coming back that if I had been more cautious, if I had told him to wear the seat belt, this would not have happened. I came across the videos of Ramesh Balsekar and you, and it is this teaching that has given me some solace. Yet, if I had been more persistent with my son and ensured that he wore the seat belt, I feel this would not have happened.

Nobody can know the pain of a parent who has lost their child. But the fact that you have found your way to this teaching and it has given you some solace, means that you were meant to find it.

If we objectively look at this situation, we can see how the sense of 'doership' is so ingrained in us: 'If I had done this, it would not have happened,' 'If I had not done that, it would not have happened,' and so on. It's all either—'I "did" something' or 'I "did not do" something'. And our whole life goes by, between all this doing and not doing.

If you were to ask yourself, 'What did I do from the moment of his birth that kept him alive?' what would be the answer? Would you be able to conclude that it was all your doing that kept him alive all those years? As we all know, God can take anyone's life away at any point.

Let us look at this from another perspective. Who built the road on which the car drove? Who invented the seat belt? Who decided that your son should leave at a particular time from a particular place and be at that very spot where the incident happened, and who decided that the oncoming car leaves at the particular time it did, and reach that same spot at the exact time the incident happened? Who decided all that? Did you decide all that? If the ego is taking ownership of the fact that because— I did not tell him this, this happened—what about all these factors that have come together to make the incident happen? This, of course, is a very unfortunate and extreme case, but we can see in our own lives that every minute of the day is linked to so many aspects totally beyond our control.

Now, what happens when there is a full understanding that one does not have control over the event? The suffering in terms of grief does not go away, but the suffering that is layered over the original suffering disappears. So it is pure grief. It is grief which will be felt fully without the extra baggage of blame, condemnation, guilt and shame, because these are the antics of the ego. Nobody guarantees one a life without suffering. The basis of life is pleasure and pain. We are here to look at life, with understanding, and minimise our suffering. As the Buddha said, 'Enlightenment is the end of suffering.'

The understanding cannot take away the grief, but it provides the solace that this could not have happened if it was not God's Will. Regret may arise that you could have been more persistent about wearing the seat belt, but it will not translate to guilt and shame.

———————

I am newly married. Our family was travelling in the car that I was driving. We had an accident in which my wife died. A thought keeps coming to my mind: If I had not driven rashly—which I don't think I had in any case—my wife would not have died. This thought is disturbing me tremendously. Can you please help?

What has happened is an actual event which will most certainly cause tremendous grief and trauma, but the event has got overlaid with a thinking mind that has started holding itself accountable and answerable for what happened. So all your time is going into thinking—'If only I had not driven the car, if only I could have avoided that accident, if only …, if only …' and so on, and the mind is going into a tailspin of depression.

But if we look objectively—which I understand is hard in such a scenario—at the factors which were needed to come together for the accident to happen and for only one person out of the four in the car to have lost her life, it becomes clear that it could not have happened if it was not the will of the Divine.

The genesis of this event can be difficult to trace; it could have begun a long time ago. For example, the road had to be there for you to be able to drive on it, the wheel had to be invented for the cars to be invented ... and so on. Did you do that? What were the factors involved that morning when you set out in your car? Who actually decided who will be in the car and who will sit where in the car? You see, there are so many factors that were not decided by us; not in our control.

This simple investigation is not just a matter of trying to give comfort to someone. This is an attempt to show them that there is truly very little in our control. And when such a setback happens, it could only happen if it was meant to.

And then, what would happen after that? If this understanding sunk in deeply, from that point on, whenever the thought arises of the loss—because grief is bound to arise—that is human nature, it is no longer overlaid with guilt and shame, and hatred for oneself. Space is created for grief simply to 'be'.

And that is why Maharaj said that one should try not to run away from pain, but to accept it and then see that it can take you to places very deep—because, to accept pain is to deny the self (which is the small self, the 'me' with the sense of 'doership'). Our immediate reaction is to avoid pain. But to accept pain is to go deeper, and when you live in the moment with your grief, you are accepting it. You are not running away from it.

We all experience loss at some point in our life—that of a person, situation, piece of property, and so on. What is the best approach with regards to experiencing loss or even the possibility or thought of loss?

Everyone's journey is a journey of loss. To lose, in order to find who you truly are. To lose, to find that which cannot be lost.

You see, my journey began when I lost my father at the age of 14. That was my first experience of a physical loss, of death. From a young age, to be exposed to death gave a heightened sense of being watchful about death. In the years that followed, this fear associated with death arose whenever I got the news of someone dying. It could be the news of the death of relatives, former colleagues at work, parents of friends, and so on. I had this heightened awareness, if you will, related to death. And with every loss, it felt like a part of me was dying. So the investigation for me began very early, into what is this loss, which scares me, as also almost everyone else?

As you say, this loss is not just the loss of people, it could be the loss of things—'objects'—in life. You lost a valuable object; you treasured something and it broke or someone stole it. Loss. Or it could be a relationship. You had a cherished friendship and your friend fought with you and parted ways. Loss. Or it could be the loss of a certain way of thinking, because you had a dramatic experience which made you relinquish your position that you held so dearly, on a particular subject. Loss. Life teaches one about loss every time.

The understanding dawned that when it is 'me' and 'mine', that is when the loss is felt most. My dog died after living a healthy life of 17 years. 'My dog'; not a stray dog on the street that died, but my dog, who used to sit near the door and welcome me every evening, when I got home from work. One day, he was gone. And I felt a vacuum; when I came home I felt his absence. The form that used to be there had vanished. Now, that vacuum felt like an external vacuum, of the absence of an external object, but the vacuum is actually felt 'inside'. I then realised that what one loses points to this emptiness. Whatever is lost, is felt within as a loss. Why is it felt as a loss? Because there is nothing there now.

If everything was stripped away from you, was taken away, you would be empty. There would be nothing to associate yourself with. I went even deeper into this investigation. I came to the conclusion that this feeling arose only when one considered what was lost as—'mine'. In other words, what one was identified with. So, if one was not identified with anything, would there even be anything as a loss felt inside, I wondered.

After a year or so of my dog's passing, my grandmother passed away. She was ailing and had been in the hospital for some days. It was during this time that I was to meet Eckhart Tolle and his group in Chennai, to travel with them to Pondicherry and Ramana Maharshi's ashram in Tiruvannamalai. We knew my grandma wasn't going to make it, but I was in a dilemma—should I cancel my trip because she was in the ICU or should I go ahead because I had confirmed that I would be there? My grandma passed away the night before I was to go on the trip. The funeral took place the next morning. I then caught the plane to Chennai.

One evening, in Pondicherry, I asked this question to Eckhart over dinner: 'When we lose loved ones, when we lose things we cherish, my understanding is because we derive our sense of self from them, we feel that loss. So if we did not derive our sense of self from them, then would we feel that loss?' I then continued to say that what one did feel was a vacuum, an emptiness. He kept listening, as if giving me a chance to air all my thoughts. I then said to him, 'So the next question that I would like you to help me with, to answer, is that as a young man the thought would come about what would happen if everyone I loved, everything I cherished, died at the same time—would there be this vacuum all around? Not just with one loss, but with 'everything' lost. And he replied, 'That is what enlightenment is,' with a smile on his face.

Emptiness is not a negative word. When one is empty, one is full of pure being. Not being this or that, but simply being. Loss is a painful yet beautiful gift; it is the taking away or stripping away of all that is required in order for the Divine light of pure being to shine in its pristine purity. On the personal level it is painful to lose a loved one, which is inevitable on the journey of life. We lose our parents sooner or later. That is the way life is designed—to learn from loss and experience loss. But for the spiritual seeker, the investigation goes further, and questions arise such as, 'What is loss? What does it point to?' 'Who is experiencing the loss?' 'Who am I prior to the loss, during the loss, and after the loss?' and so on.

Now, what about the other kinds of loss? What happens when you lose your thoughts of judgements, lose your criticism, lose your hatred and malice, lose your blame and condemnation, lose your guilt and shame, lose all thoughts of 'doership' that make these feelings arise? Once again, what is left is the vast peace of being that can never be lost. That is what is yours. It is not yours as an object, but rather who you truly are, in your true essence. That is the gift of the teaching. You can only lose what you are not, you can never lose what you are.

That is your true wealth. Your true wealth is truly no thing, which is yet everything because that does not leave you. How can pure being leave you? This thought itself brings about healing.

———

If one has accepted the transient nature of life and one is generally more at peace now, is there a difference between, say, not getting your favourite chocolate versus losing someone you love?

Love for the chocolate is because of the pleasure it has given, through the sense of taste. It is a pleasure dependent on a sense; one of five senses. If the desire arises to have your favourite chocolate and it is not available at hand, then one understands that this desire arose but was not meant to be fulfilled, at this moment. Pursuing the desire for that chocolate will not happen beyond a point. The desire arose, but whether the desire is fulfilled or not is God's Will; this is the understanding in operation.

Love for someone is a deeper bond, in that sense. Rivers of love are karmic in nature. What happens when one loses someone one loves? Most certainly, grief will arise. We are human beings, it is in our nature to grieve the loss of a loved one. But for the sage, that grief will not be extended in the duration of horizontal time, into mourning.

Let's say some time has passed by, after the loss of a dear one. One evening, you go to the movies with some friends and the memory arises of having been there, at the movie hall, with your loved one. This brings up sadness. Moments of sadness are bound to be there. But that will not be stretched into a story— 'I should not have lost my loved one!' 'Why did God do this to me?' 'How cruel is God!' 'What have I done wrong to people that this has been my destiny?' This dialogue of the thinking mind stops. Then, what is experienced is simply pure grief, in the moment.

In both cases—that of not getting your favourite chocolate and losing a loved one—the dialogue of the thinking mind stops. That is what they have in common.

An important point to note is that many of us relentlessly pursue our desires to the extent that we cause suffering upon ourselves and others. This does not happen for the sage as he lives 'in the moment', in vertical time.

SPIRITUAL PATHS AND PRACTICES

'There is no point in enjoying a spiritual practice that does not permeate one's daily living.'

Can you please suggest a technique to practice?

The mind loves techniques, simply because it is accustomed to 'doing'. Therefore, you should do what you feel you want to do.

It is not easy to sit still. Nisargadatta Maharaj said that we keep making use of consciousness to conduct various activities, but rarely do we stay established as Consciousness. This is the paradox—we love our consciousness so much; we love to 'be'. Yet, we find just 'being' unbearable, so we end up constantly wanting to do something or the other. Even if it means going for a walk, watching a movie, or sipping a cup of coffee.

This teaching operates on its own, without you having to 'do' something. It is in the nature of an understanding that comes up during the course of one's life. Once exposed to it, it is like a new conditioning that replaces the earlier conditioning, Therefore, there is no technique as such to practice.

Once, a boy familiar with the talks came to me saying, 'I am in "working mind" mode from morning to evening.' You see, in one of my earlier talks I gave this example that my teacher often gave, of a surgeon doing a surgery. While it is happening, he (the surgeon) is totally focussed on the operation, with his years of experience guiding him. His 'working mind' is active. But let's say someone tells him that the patient being operated on is a politician so he better be careful, then his 'thinking mind' could become active. The thinking mind strays into an imaginary future—'I better be careful. If something doesn't go quite right with the surgery, my career could be at stake.'

Coming back to the boy, when I asked him what the nature of his work was, that kept him in the 'working mind' mode all day, he replied that he kept himself busy playing video games so that his thinking mind was not active. This is exactly the point—one knows how the thinking mind gallops into the dead past or an imaginary future all the time, not leaving one in peace. Yet, the alternative is seen to be to stay in 'working mind' mode all the time, which can be quite draining. For, one is afraid of the mind being still. Because a still mind is perceived as a dead mind. But it is quite a beautiful space to be in—one that allows witnessing to happen. This is Conscious Presence. Then, if the thought arises to be engaged in some activity, one honours that. If this does not arise, one is content with 'being'. There is no longer the compulsion to keep the mind engaged constantly, be it 'working mind' or 'thinking mind'.

Of course, this can only 'happen'. One cannot force the mind to be still, as it would only take one further away as the stillness that is sought is nothing but the absence of 'doing'.

———————

I have done practically everything for the last 20 years. I have attended Vedanta classes, done hypnotherapy, past life regression, Kriya yoga, study of scriptures and so on. How do I know whether I have found my path?

Firstly, the fact is that if you are still trying things out, it means you have not found it. But, more importantly, do you know what it is that you are looking for? How will you find something—in this case, your path—unless you know what it is that you are looking for? You have to ask yourself this question. Deep down, one knows what one is looking for is peace of mind.

Quite right. Now that I know that I am looking for peace of mind, what next?

One has to do exactly what one thinks and feels one should do to get peace of mind. That is the journey of seeking. On that journey, which was not started by you in the first place, you have to trust the same Force that started it to lead you to your destination. Depending on your destiny you will come across something, some teaching, practice, or someone, which will trigger within you the peace and you will recognise that that is where your place is, that is where you belong, that is where you feel most at home. Then you do not have the need to move around anymore. The journey thereafter becomes a conscious one.

Ultimately, external movement is just an expression of internal movement. It is the moving mind which gets externalised by going to various places and doing various things. When the thinking mind (the internal movement) starts subsiding one rests in the stillness, the peace of mind, more and more.

Is there such a thing as diksha in non-duality and if so, do you give it?
It is the initiation into peace, which itself is the diksha, because all
of us, whether we know it or not, are looking for peace of mind.
And this teaching shows the way to that peace. The teaching
itself is the initiation and living the teaching is its gift. It is not
the teaching of one body initiating another, it is Consciousness
initiating Itself through recognition of Itself.

Having said that, sometimes masters like Nisargadatta Maharaj
gave the *naam mantra* (repetition of the sacred name) to some
disciples, seeing their temperament and mental make-up. Giving
the naam mantra could be considered as diksha, in their case.

---

*Why are we supposed to learn only from suffering, why not from
pleasures?*
Suffering is generally the suffering of a loss; we suffer because we
feel we are losing something—that which we are identified with.
All suffering is because the 'me' feels threatened and diminished.
'Me and my story' is in deep threat; that is why one suffers. 'What
will happen to me? I will die.' This applies to physical as well as
psychological suffering. This is why the Buddhists say that all
suffering is eventually nothing but the fear of death.

The stripping away of whatever one is identified with, brings
on suffering, but this is also the start of the spiritual journey. The
questions then arise: 'Who is the "me" that suffers? Who am I,
when I am not identified with anything?'

We learn from pleasures too, for we learn that pleasures do not last. They are transient, and a temporary happiness is derived from them. Life is not just moments of pleasure, but in fact, many moments of pleasures and pain. Generally, our lives are filled with more moments of pain than pleasure.

When does the running after pleasures stop?

The natural course of life's experiences and subsequent learning is to come to the conclusion that pleasures are transient. So you keep seeing that when you run after pleasure, you enjoy it for some time, and then you start looking for the next pleasure. You are actually seeking yourself in something transient. So it's a natural mechanism, especially when you are younger, to seek pleasure after pleasure, and each pleasure is the harbinger of pain, which is your life's experience. For example, you fall in love with someone, you find someone in your youth, and then there is pain afterwards. You then realise it was only lust or infatuation, but there was no bond of a deeper nature.

When the realisation dawns, there comes a natural understanding that 'my happiness which is dependent on pleasures is not a lasting happiness'. True happiness cannot depend on a pleasure, because pleasures are cheats. Then the spiritual journey begins and one wonders, 'Can I get that true happiness without running after pleasures? What kind of happiness would that be?' And one reaches the conclusion that true happiness is nothing but peace of mind.

Earlier the focus is projected outwards, on what I perceive as outside me, from which I derived pleasure. Now the focus reverses gear and turns within. That is the start of the spiritual journey.

Another point to note is that in the moment of heightened pleasure, there is no 'me'. The 'me' steps in later and claims it as 'my' experience, and so starts wanting more of it. Then the frustration begins as one hankers after experiences to gain pleasure from. Seeing the futility of this, sometimes the search begins, the search to look for that which does not depend on an experience, and which is permanent. This is the search for true happiness.

True happiness is the peace of 'being'. The peace of 'being' is where you come and rest, not 'becoming'. If objects are enjoyed, they are enjoyed with the full knowledge and understanding that while they are there, the enjoyment is there. Make no mistake—it does not mean walking away from pleasures, but the understanding is now completely different. Knowing that everything is transient, there is no incessant seeking for pleasure after pleasure. If something presents itself or there is a natural desire for something you like doing, it happens spontaneously. But the dependency on seeking pleasure after pleasure starts withdrawing. That is why Maharaj said, 'Between the banks of pain and pleasure the river of life flows.' But the problem with us is that we want only the bank of pleasure. It is not possible.

Many teachers talk about surrender. What is surrender? What does it mean to be surrendered? Does humility arise spontaneously from this state?

What we can truly surrender is only what is ours. But what is ours? Nothing. We come into this world with nothing and we leave with nothing. When they say we must surrender, what are they pointing at? There is nothing that is mine as such. So the only thing to surrender is the sense of 'doership'. That is the true surrender.

What we do is 'we' try to surrender; 'I' must surrender. The true surrender is the absence of the 'me' who wants to surrender. But we have taken ownership of the surrender itself. If I surrender to this situation, I will be fine. Do you have a choice? The circumstance has already chosen you. So, to reiterate, true surrender is the absence of the 'me' that wants to surrender. Then you are no longer in this mode of 'I must accept this, I must surrender;' and so on. That dialogue is gone because the acceptance of 'what is', is already there. Surrender has already happened, without the 'me' sitting on top of it saying, 'I have surrendered'.

That is why Rameshji would say that one cannot choose to be humble, because to choose to be humble is yet another step away from being humble. To choose to be humble means the 'me' wants to be humble; yet another attribute to add to 'my' qualities. True humility is not recognised as such by the one who has it.

So this whole notion of 'I want to surrender' or 'I surrender' is a set-up. It's a trap. Acceptance of 'what is' is true surrender. Surrender to the Source of all there is. Thy Will be done.

———

I have a question about surrender. In 'Pointers from Ramesh Balsekar' you say that the only thing we have to surrender to God is our sense of 'personal doership'. However, you also say that our personal will is ultimately God's Will. Whatever I decide to do in a given situation is exactly what God wants me to do. So, could it be said that we have already surrendered to God without even trying? Everyone is doing what they think is best, according to their genes and conditioning. So is it even possible for someone to not be surrendered to God? Please help me to understand how surrender fits into this teaching.

A wonderful and well thought out question. I am glad you are delving deeply into the teachings.

Yes, our personal will is ultimately God's Will because the decisions we take are based on our genetics and conditioning, two factors that are not in our control.

We are not surrendered to God when there is hatred, malice, jealousy, envy, blame, condemnation, guilt, shame, pride, arrogance and so on. If we were surrendered to God, which means a total acceptance that no one is the doer of their actions (neither me nor others) except God—the Source, then these would not arise. And if these would not arise, then we would be truly surrendered to God 'without even trying', as you say.

The degree of peace, harmony, tranquility we experience in our lives is directly proportional to the degree of our surrender, one could say.

Is it possible to have two gurus?

At one level, one can have as many gurus as one likes. Lord Dattatreya had 24 gurus. You may pick up something from one guru and something different from another guru. But if you have two gurus, you need to ask yourself, 'Where do I feel more at home? Where do I feel more at peace?' If one is established in peace, then even the doubt of which one is your guru will not arise.

The risk of having many gurus is that one is 'acquiring'— acquiring from here and there, acquiring knowledge, and so on, whereas the function of the guru is that of stripping away. So when you feel, 'Now I do not need to go anywhere else', that is a pointer. You feel, 'Now I am tired. I want to rest in one place and hear my favourite song all the time'.

When Rameshji was asked this question, he would reply by saying that one could have more than one guru, but at a given point of time one can have only one guru. At another point in your journey, you could consider someone else as your guru. He was talking from his personal experience. When Nisargadatta Maharaj was asked this question, he replied by saying that to find water, one doesn't need to dig many shallow wells all over the place, but rather, one deep well.

How does one know if a specific teacher is one's guru?

When someone asked Rameshji, 'Are you my guru?' he replied, 'It all depends. If you are my disciple, then I am your guru.' Gurus do not go around proclaiming themselves as gurus. The decision belongs to the student/disciple, for it is the disciple who makes the guru. The guru is content in his ordinariness, or you could say, extra-ordinariness. He does not even need the label of 'guru'.

When Ramana Maharshi was asked about how one recognises whether a sage is a true sage, he replied that it is by the degree of peace and sense of respect one feels for him.

Ultimately, the guru-disciple relationship is a bond forged by destiny. It is really not a 'choice' made by the disciple, though it might appear to be so.

If enlightenment is enlightenment, then why is it that every enlightened teacher's experience is different?

Because they are different people. Jesus was different from Lord Ram. It is bound to be, that is the nature of manifestation. They grew up in different environments, in different times, with different genetics, with a specific set of circumstances in each case, and so on. That is why we have many enlightened masters and many paths.

But, more importantly, enlightenment is not an 'experience'. Let's take an example from our own daily living. No matter who we are, what our paths are, what we do during the day, what our conditioning is, what our life circumstances are, is my deep sleep different from yours? It cannot be. Degree of sleep may vary, but deep sleep is the same. Deep sleep is deep sleep, just like you say enlightenment is enlightenment. What I am pointing to is the impersonal consciousness. Impersonal consciousness in the deep sleep state (I do not know that I exist) and identified consciousness in the waking state and the dream state (I am so and so). Two sides of the same coin. The personalities that exist in the waking state differ, but what happens to them in deep sleep?

Anyone in this room would have their own experience of their 'journey to' enlightenment, even if they follow the same teacher or guru. Their experience along the journey will not be the same. It is your own journey. And because of this, a beautifully unique journey it is.

Can siddhi powers be real?
Siddhi powers can be real, but ultimately only as real as the illusion they are a part of. That is why Nisargadatta Maharaj's guru forbade him from performing 'siddhis' which he sometimes did in the initial stages, to help people.

According to me, the most underrated siddhi is living a life of peace and harmony, like a sea of calm.

Is the action of yantras, icons and amulets akin to the placebo effect, based on one's belief in its effectiveness?

If the yantras, amulets and icons are energised by someone qualified to energise them, who has the full knowledge of the esoteric sciences, then yes, they can have an impact. But ultimately, they will work only if it is God's Will.

I am a 26-year-old postgraduate student. Please tell me what one should do on a daily basis to attain liberation from the cycle of birth and death?

Let's begin with working towards peace of mind in daily living, and leave the issue of liberation to God. What I speak and write about has this specific focus on peace of mind in daily living.

Do different people following different paths have different spiritual experiences, and how does it matter?

There are so many experiences of and within Consciousness. If you read Gorakhnath's books, he will take you through all of them. Different people following different paths may or may not have spiritual experiences. They may be the same, they may be different, but at the end of the day what they have in common is that they are experiences.

But more importantly, what is your life's expression right now? Is it one of peace or is it one of conflict? Because you may have all the spiritual experiences you like, but of what use are they if your life is still one where you are not at peace?

Our scriptures are full of stories of yogis who have faltered on the path. In moments of anger, things have been said and done which they have then regretted. Supposing God came to you and said that He will give you experiences of many levels of samadhi, but your daily living might be full of strife and conflict in relationships, or you could choose a life of complete peace with what happens, but without the experiences—which of the two options would you choose?

As the Buddha said, 'Samsara is dukkha. Nirvana is shanti.'

When Maharaj said, 'I do not make disciples, I make gurus,' he was not referring to gifting the disciples the various states of samadhi and consciousness that would make them gurus. His whole teaching was to 'abide in one's being' because if one lives that, then one lives as a guru, not in the sense of a guru with disciples but rather the guru principle, as Consciousness—which is the meaning of the word 'guru'.

Why does it take so much time to know ourselves if we are 'That'?
It is the thinking mind that asks this question, because it lives in the dead past or the imaginary future. The thinking mind operates in horizontal time, as my teacher used to say. We are 'That' in vertical time, in the now. The thinking mind wants to know how much time it will take to know its own absence!

Does 'oneness' mean that I will live everyone else's life? The idea that everyone around me is really just 'me' is highly disturbing.

Consciousness functions through different human beings like electricity functions through different household appliances. Just as the electrical juicer is programmed to produce a different output from the toaster, similarly each individual body-mind organism is programmed differently—as a result of genetics and conditioning—to produce a specific output. We are instruments through whom the same energy functions.

Therefore, to answer your question, 'Everyone is really me' in the sense that it is the same Consciousness that functions through the different 'mes'. However, each 'me' lives his life as a separate 'me'. Therefore, the question of living another 'me's' life does not arise, just as the juicer cannot perform the same function as the toaster.

At a deeper level of understanding, it means that Consciousness is all there is; there truly are no others to be separate from. We are not living our lives but rather are 'being lived', just as the gadgets in the kitchen are 'being lived' by the electricity that functions through them.

––––––––––

In one of your books it is written: 'Read the Bhagavad Gita from the perspective of Krishna'. What do you mean by that?

That is what the sage Nisargadatta Maharaj used to say. His whole teaching was that 'you are not the body'. So what he is saying is, don't read the Gita from an individual perspective. Read it as if you are the pure light of Consciousness reading the book. In other words, if you were not conscious, you could not read the Gita. So read it from that perspective and not from the twisted judgements and views of the individual 'me'—an individual identified with the name and form of his body. Read it from the perspective of the 'Universal Consciousness'—Krishna. Do not read it from the perspective of the identified ego consciousness.

Then that should go for anything and everything, shouldn't it?

If you can live like that, then that is 'awakened' living. If you are free from resentments, ill-will, spite, hatred, jealousy, pride, arrogance, guilt and shame—the game is up. But if you 'think' you are free from all that, then the game is not up. *(Laughter)*

Would you elaborate on the concept of God?

For most of us, God is an object—one which we pray to. More often than not, that prayer is in the form of begging, asking God to do this or that for us. That is not the God being referred to here. The God being referred to is Consciousness. If you were not conscious, you could not worship any God. So who are you referring to when you say God? Is it the God that is within your consciousness as an object? Or the 'Consciousness' which one calls God? Some people don't like the word 'God' because of a lot of conditioning associated with it, so 'Consciousness' is a more appropriate word. It is the Source without which there is nothing— no you, me, he or she.

But you say there is a plan, and it's working according to His will.
Well, it's not working according to your will. If it did, then everything you did in life would go your way. So, it is working according to the will of the Source.

But the Source resides in you, right?
The Source does not reside in you; it is you who reside in the Source. *(Laughter)* We actually got disconnected from the Source, because it was the will of the Source. The Source wants to reconnect to Itself through us.

Then why do you use the words 'God' and 'Source'? Why not use the word 'Consciousness'?
Because if I keep using the word 'Consciousness', my tongue will get tired. *(Laughter)*

Some people don't like the concept of God.
You know, my teacher used to say that an atheist can be an atheist only if it is God's Will. *(Laughter)* On a more serious note, if he was not conscious he would not be an atheist. So the teaching keeps pointing back to Consciousness.

Does denying God mean that there is a God to deny?
Obviously. That is the first sign of God. The sage Ramana Maharshi once told his audience: 'There is no free will.' One person put

up his hand and said, 'I put up my hand, so that's my free will.' Sri Ramana said, 'Of course not! If I had not said that there is no free will, you would not have put up your hand!'

What tools would you recommend to the audience to lessen this duality, to be less fragmented?

No tools. Who wants the tools? The mind—more specifically, the 'thinking mind'! So please don't get involved in trying to be a witness, because the ego cannot witness.

I am not sure why I am writing this to you and whether you would reply. I am restless. Reading books and browsing videos of spiritual masters seems to have become a habit, an obsession. Some say there is nothing to be done; others say something must be done. To look for the sense of 'I am' is what I try to do these days, but I am not sure if that is the way for me. 'Is there a need for the presence of a teacher?' This question is bothering me. I am not even sure if I truly have the desire to understand myself, or is it just an escape from daily problems? I stumbled upon your videos today and thought you might know what is really going on, and help me. I will be grateful if I can get a pointer from you.

What you have stated is the plight of many spiritual seekers. The consolation is that you did not start the seeking in the first place; God did. So let the path unfold as per His plan.

Generally, what I have observed is that such confusion arises because we don't know what we are looking for. But it is clear that what every human being is looking for, whether he knows it or not, is peace of mind.

Therefore, I would suggest following that path or finding a teacher who shows you the way to peace of mind in daily living. For what could be more important than that?

The point you raised in your mail is important: 'I am not even sure if I truly have the desire to understand myself or is it just an escape from daily problems?' The truth is that only you would know whether you are escaping from daily problems, or whether you are facing them, and at the same time, also seeking a balm (in the form of a teacher or teaching) that will help you face such situations with equanimity.

I can't say whether the presence of a teacher would be 'essential' in your case, but I am sure it would help the process. I was in the physical presence of my teacher and for me it was essential. I think it was essential for my teacher as well, that is, to be with his teacher.

All the best for the unfolding of your spiritual journey—it is not something to be dreaded. Consider your glass half full and not half empty.

As suggested by you, I contemplated on what I really want. I am convinced now that it is the search for peace of mind and may be happiness. But peace of mind, a feeling of being content, seems to resonate more. So far, my main motive was to achieve the feeling of being someone special. I am now probably clearer about what it was, and what it is. Writing to you about the confusion in my mind helped put me at ease. I am now more convinced that things are happening, and that I am not the one who is making them happen. Thank you so much for being there for me.

Peace of mind is the true happiness as it is not a happiness that depends on momentary pleasures. Yes, the ego indeed wants to be special. That has now been seen clearly. Thanking me is like your left hand thanking your right hand.

It has been some time since I last wrote to you. Moments of silence are happening to me these days. Sometimes, when I am trying to be one with the feeling of 'I am', I can't seem to do it. My mind goes on chattering. However, at times the silence pops up spontaneously. Sometimes, in that silence, my attention gets locked on to some part of the brain, the forehead, the right side of the brain or on my nose. Though I try to move it or unlock it, I cannot seem to consciously do it. After some time, my focus or attention seems to go off on its own. I do not understand what it is, why it is, and how to deal with it. Could you please say something about it?

Like you have said, when you try to be one with the 'I am', you can't do it. That's precisely the point. It is this very 'you' with its sense of 'doership' that tries too hard to be its own absence, so that the Presence shines through. Yes, the 'silence' indeed pops up spontaneously without you having to do anything.

Now, regarding the experience of your attention getting locked on to some part of the brain—as long as it happens on its own, without you trying to induce it, let it play its part in the process of unfoldment. As you have said, it goes off on its own after some time. The Creative Force has infinite intelligence and does not require 'you' to 'do' anything with it; it will take its natural course.

Thank you. I could not have shared all this with anyone else. I feel really blessed to have your guidance. I can now see that the trying itself prevents the 'silence'. When the mind is very active and there is no sense of separation from it, then I feel very frustrated. What would be the best course of action at such times? Also, I never used to wake up early. Since the past week, there is an urge to wake up early in the morning and sit in silence. I feel like doing this even in the evening. On my way home from the office, I have found a quiet place in a garden, where I can sit and contemplate. This appears strange even to me, but I am doing it. I will continue doing it as long as there is the urge. I will keep reporting further about such happenings, to you.

When the mind is very active, it is the understanding that comes forth and cuts off the involvement. If one keeps trying to 'do' something to cut off the involvement and one is not successful, it can lead to frustration. To 'do' something to cut off the involvement could mean getting further 'involved' in the involvement.

Many people underrate the value of sitting in silence, but it is the best practice. It is nice to know that it is 'happening' for you. As you said, continue doing it until the urge is there.

Thank you for taking the time out of your busy schedule to reply. You have been very kind to me. I want to tell you about the experience

I had today. I am hesitant, because I don't know if it was really happening. I was doing something but there was also an internal dialogue going on about what I am and who the 'me' really is, and all that. I happened to look at the wall in front of me and, somehow, I felt that I was hollow inside—meaning, that there was nothing inside me. I felt that the wall in front of me and my body were in a field of something, and they were both appearing in that field. I felt that there was some distance between the wall and me, but I was not sure if it can really be called a 'distance'. Everything had a jelly-like texture. It was not feeling solid. But when I touched the wall, I could feel it was solid to the touch. There was also something inside me saying, 'What is this happening? Is there nothing in my brain as "me"?' Does this mean my mind is 'empty' now? I am now confused. Was this kind of made up by my mind because I have been reading or hearing about it? But surely, I can't be mistaking that feeling. Can you please guide me?'

What you have described is known as 'witnessing'. The fact that you say, 'I was doing something and also internal dialogue was going on about what is "me" and all that' means that there was awareness of it all. In other words, all phenomena were witnessed.

The world is not out there; it appears within our consciousness. For if we were not conscious, there would be no world.

Sitting in silence for some time and meditation—which is the simple awareness of being—would be beneficial. Witnessing means observing all that arises—thoughts, feelings, emotions—without judging.

I was eagerly waiting for your response. More things are unfolding since last week and I am feeling so much gratitude. It's almost like I am thanking everything and everyone around for what has been happening. I was not sure what that experience was when I wrote to you, but now, with your confirmation, I can say that things are happening as they are meant to happen. Right now when I write this, my mind is almost switched off. If it can happen to me, no word other than 'Grace' comes to my mind to explain it. It happens at its will and I can only witness it, and thank it. I do not know what is going to happen next, but I am now sure that it will be what it has to be. I want to remain in silence because I cannot explain to anyone else what is happening. Probably this is how it is supposed to happen.

Gratitude to God is perhaps the only genuine prayer. Wanting to thank everyone and everything around you is akin to thanking God—for God, or Consciousness, is all there is.

'Grace' is indeed the right word.

Nisargadatta Maharaj said that one has to be convinced that he is not the body. In one particular talk, he said, 'Like a body is being cremated, it is gone. You have to be convinced like that.' Is the conviction of not being the body sufficient to stop the cycle of birth and death? Or does one have to realise the Self ... and awaken?

According to my understanding, the conviction that you are not the body is the 'awakening'. It is the 'Total Conviction', and not just an intellectual conviction.

130

After this, there is no 'one' to be concerned with the cycle of birth and death.

Is perfect happiness the same as perfect self-realisation? And, how can I know for sure whether I'm truly on the spiritual path or just deluded? If it's the latter, how do I overcome it?

Yes. Self-realisation manifests as true (I wouldn't use the word 'perfect') happiness, which is *sukha-shanti*.

The way you will know for sure whether you're truly on the spiritual path is by the degree of peace you feel. If you feel more peaceful than before, then it is a good indicator. The 'delusion' would be to 'think' that one is at peace, though one does not feel peace within.

DEVOTION
TO GOD

'True bhakti is to see the presence of God in all the people we come across, especially those we don't like.'

Why do forms of Gods and Goddesses and temples exist in so many cultures?

We are in the world of form so it is much easier for us to relate to a form of God. That is why these forms were created—to be worshipped, which is the bhakti tradition. Each form represents an aspect of the Divine, which is in truth not apart from us. The Advaita tradition is one of worshipping the formless God, formless Consciousness. So in one, it is a relationship between me and God, and in the other, the 'I Am', the formless Consciousness, the 'Being', is God.

But all these questions are fine as long as your sincerity and earnestness is focused on one aspect, which is peace of mind. Because there is no end to the questions that the mind can raise. But if you hold on to that one point of focus, that very focus will gift you that peace. The mind is made to ask questions. There is a whole science behind building temples and cathedrals that we don't know anything about. They were built by master builders and craftsmen, who knew how to symbolically represent levels of consciousness. There is nothing to negate in it; we only display our ignorance when we do so. I raise this point because many on the path of Jnana Yoga look down upon people who visit temples.

What is devotion to God? Like, if someone asks 'What is "tea"?', it can be described as an aromatic beverage prepared with tea leaves immersed in hot water, and so on. Similarly, what is actually meant by devotion? What will be our thoughts if we are truly devoted?

'Devotion to God' simply means your love for God. Regarding your question, 'What will be our thoughts if we are truly devoted?' the answer is that all thoughts will be directed towards God.

If you are on the bhakti path, the form of God you relate to (Shiva/Ganesha, etc.) would be foremost on your mind and in your consciousness throughout the day. After all, one wants to be with the one that one loves, all the time.

If one is truly devoted, one would see the presence of God in all the people we come across, including those we don't like. God has assumed all the forms. Everyone is an instrument of the Divine.

What is devotion to God? My parents say that I am doing something wrong by not doing puja and rituals, by not praying before the deity. I recently came across the teaching of Nisargadatta Maharaj which did not make any sense to me, yet I felt calm. I could not understand why. And subsequently I found your videos and it drew me to this teaching. I do not understand devotion as my parents understand it, so what is devotion to God in this teaching? Please tell me, in simple words.

Simply put, devotion to God is devotion to peace of mind in daily living. How so? It is quite simple. All you have to do is to enquire what disturbs your peace during the day. And you will realise invariably that it is a thought of something someone has 'done', either someone else or yourself. 'Why did he do this to me?', Why did she say this to me?', 'How dare he say that to me?', and the pursuant blame, condemnation, hatred, envy, jealousy, malice, guilt, shame, and so on. These thoughts disturb the peace.

But if you accept that everyone—like yourself, is an instrument of God, conditioned by the way God conditioned them, right from childhood—you realise that people are precisely the way God has made them. And with that understanding, thoughts which were crowding one's mind start dropping off. The thinking mind which is so active, going into the imaginary future or the dead past, starts disengaging. Then the pure Presence which is always there, which was earlier covered by the thinking mind, starts shining through. So life is now lived with presence. One starts 'abiding in one's being', as a natural outcome of this, not as a method. And that is why Maharaj, when asked, 'Why do you not advocate worshipping Shiva, Ganesha?' replied something along the lines of, 'Because they would not exist if your sense of being were not there. They exist in your mind because you "are".' So who is God? Your sense of being or an object in your consciousness? When you abide in your being, you are worshipping God.

Sometimes, people who are on the bhakti path have an intense love for God, for the personal deity they worship. However, their personal relationships are in a mess. They do not get along with siblings, they fight with colleagues, and have relationships that are not harmonious. Now, the understanding that no one truly does anything transforms these relationships. So you are living with this worship throughout the day, worshipping the same Consciousness that functions through everyone. This is a living ritual and not an action being performed.

You may not be performing a ritual, but you now know that just as there are different gadgets in the kitchen, each designed to produce what it is designed to, but without electricity they are all dead objects that cannot function, similarly, it is the same Consciousness that animates all of us but each is designed a certain way, they think and perform actions a certain way, the way they have been designed according to their genetics and conditioning. What happens with this understanding is that you stop taking things personally, in a way. It's no longer 'me versus the other', which has been your mantra so far. It now shifts to 'me and the other', whoever the other may be; right from a family member to a stranger on the street.

One starts losing one's sense of preference of who is closer and who is not, because one is seeing with an even vision. That is why the sages do not discriminate between someone who has been with them for many years and someone who has just come into their presence, because they are not looking at individuals as such.

Their sight has moved beyond the gadgets to the Presence, to the electricity.

———————

I have deep faith in God but at times it tends to waver, and when that happens I doubt myself. Why does this happen?

Faith wavers, in general, when things do not go 'my' way. When things go my way, then I have full faith. So, what is the faith that does not waver? It can only be that which does not depend on whether or not things go my way.

The faith in knowing that whatever happens now or the next moment is God's Will, is the unwavering faith. Then you are aligned with whatever happens, which may be perceived as good or bad by the ego. The ego, the 'thinking mind', is what brings about the wavering. The total acceptance of 'what is', is the firm faith in God's Will operating.

Now, when that happens, it is a total annihilation of 'my' will as against God's Will. It is, quite literally, 'Not my will Oh Lord, but Thine, be done.' Then there is no question of whether or not one has faith, because you are in full alignment with 'what is', which is God-in-operation. When one has walked on a normal life path where one has seen enough disappointments, one has seen things not going one's way, one reaches the logical conclusion that the only true faith is the total acceptance that whatever happens is God's Will. Heaven is to be found in the heart of the man who has total acceptance that whatever happens is God's Will.

MEDITATION
AND
WITNESSING

'True meditation is living with the understanding
that God's Will prevails at all times.'

What can I do to steady the mind? Are there any practices that I can follow?

It is the thinking mind that incessantly jumps into the past and the future. To 'steady the mind' refers to the 'thinking mind'. And the thinking mind, which is the ego with its sense of 'doership', functions through patterns that are the outcome of one's conditioning.

These patterns are based on memories of a dead past or fears of an imaginary future. How does one break these patterns? In the waking state, patterns of the ego will repeat till they are supposed to repeat. All that can happen (I am not saying all that one can do), is that awareness is brought to the pattern. And over time, sometimes suddenly, one will notice that the pattern of the thinking mind, of going into different directions and trajectories, starts changing, starts reducing. The mind is no longer going into those zones and that is when one knows that the understanding has taken effect.

One has to just be a witness to the movements of the mind. That is what true meditation is. True meditation is not about concentration or quietening the mind with a sense of volition or 'doership'. True meditation is witnessing all the thoughts that arise in the meditation without any judgement, without saying they should not arise. In other words, witnessing whatever arises in the moment. It is just like witnessing traffic go by on the road.

It is this witnessing of the entanglements of the thinking mind, that takes place more and more. As a result of this, the thinking mind starts subsiding, till one reaches a point of stillness within. That stillness is the absence of the thinking mind. Over time, this results in more and more silence; silence on the outside and stillness on the inside. We find the need to speak less, to give our viewpoints, our opinions, less and less. As Maharaj would say, 'Speechlessness befits the great man.' He would also say, 'Realised people are very quiet.'

The need to get involved in everything that goes on, in opinions on world politics for example, in this and that ... this constant barrage of involvement through the day starts subsiding. In yoga, there is a term—the 'hamsa mudra'—where one eye is looking out into the world and the other's gaze is turned inside. There were sages who were in that state, part of the world and yet apart from it. When the thinking mind starts becoming still, more and more of 'witnessing' the events in one's life starts happening.

Doesn't meditation cause the mind—the 'thinking mind'—to go all over the place? And you can't actually do anything about it, can you?

In meditation, you are sometimes aware that your mind is going all over the place. In the waking state you are not aware. So be happy that a lot of thoughts come to your mind in meditation because you are aware that they are there. Most of us are not aware; we are just caught up in running here and there with our thoughts. The fact that you said a lot of thoughts come to you during meditation means that you were not those thoughts and, therefore, you recognised them as thoughts. People get discouraged when they realise they may get a lot of thoughts in meditation, but that's actually very good. Who knows that? Who knows that there are many thoughts coming? That is the witness. With time, the thinking will subside in meditation. In life, we are constantly taught the same lessons in order to bring them to our awareness. Once we learn something, it generally does not manifest again because the learning is complete. Your head is already in the tiger's mouth, as the first step of sitting in meditation has already been taken.

———————

You say that witnessing the mind is meditation. I am practicing self-inquiry and have in the past witnessed the mind. From what I understand about inquiry, it is to search within for the Source or the witness.

Is witnessing the same as seeking the witness? Witnessing seems more natural to me (effortless), seeking the witness takes more effort and is strained. Will witnessing lead to the dissolution of the 'I' or is inquiry required?

Yes, meditation is witnessing whatever arises as movements in Consciousness. It is like a living meditation that can't be 'practiced' as such, as it is a way of 'seeing' rather than 'doing'.

The self-inquiry you are referring to (for example, Ramana Maharshi's practice) is a specific process of inquiry. When a thought arises, one asks, 'To whom is this appearing?' If the answer should emerge—'to me', one then asks, 'Who is this me?' and so forth. This brings our attention to the 'false I', the ego, which cannot exist on its own without thoughts.

One cannot really practice self-inquiry throughout the day if one is in the thick of things (having a regular working life, for instance). Whereas, witnessing 'happens', and is the functioning of the understanding in daily living.

Yes, my understanding is that witnessing leads to the dissolution of the 'false I'. Once again, it can only happen, and can't be 'done' as such.

PRAYER

'The true prayer is a prayer of gratitude
that arises from the heart.'

I have heard that prayers can move mountains and most religions have given significance to prayers. Do prayers have the power to change God's Will or is even that according to God's Will?

It depends on what is your definition of prayer. Now, if it is a prayer for something good to happen to 'me', that is according to what I feel is good for me, it may turn out to be exactly the other way over the course of time. As the saying goes, 'Be careful what you pray for, you might just get it!' It's hard to know what is good for us, as we don't have the entire perspective.

True prayer is a prayer of gratitude. As Rameshji would say, 'Anytime you feel bad for yourself, think of millions below the poverty line and then be grateful to God that you are not in their shoes.'

In my formative years, my prayer was, 'Dear God, give me the strength to deal with life's situations and challenges.' I suppose that's because I did face many challenges in those years. Decades later, when I read a book called *Silence of the Heart* by Robert Adams, a disciple of Ramana Maharshi, I was very comforted as he mentions this very prayer.

So if you are asking about whether a prayer to want something in life—like the 'me' wanting something—will work or not, I honestly have no idea and it has not been my approach to life.

But the truest prayer is, 'Not my will Oh Lord, but Thine, be done.' That is true surrender. That is why even The Mother of Pondicherry said that one must have faith and trust in the Divine, in the will of the Divine.

There was a boy who had come to see my mother. He was about 30 years old, and he was in love with a girl. He went to the temples to pray that she come into his life, and she did. So his prayers were answered. But they split up after six months. Shirdi Sai Baba has said, 'People come to me asking me for so many things, but nobody asks me to give what I want to give them. What about what I want to give them? Everyone is coming and asking what they want!' Do we go with an empty cup in front of Sai Baba and say, 'Okay, I am all yours to fill up?' Hardly.

Yet, a prayer can arise from the heart. Supposing you see a loved one who is going through a poor health experience or financial difficulty, you feel it as your pain and a genuine prayer may arise to the Lord to lessen this person's difficulty, but know that ultimately what has to happen will happen. This understanding will not prevent a spontaneous prayer from arising. You are not going to sit and say, 'Oh, everything is God's Will, so there is no point in praying.' That becomes again an intellectual understanding. This kind of prayer does not depend on the outcome. The prayer arises on its own as a wish; not as a means to an end.

Even to wish well for oneself, is a spontaneous prayer. Why not? But if we then get focussed on what will be the outcome of the prayer, we set ourselves up for disappointment if the prayer is not answered to our liking. That is where the difficulty arises for we then say, 'God did not listen to my prayer, I prayed so hard but I did not get what I wanted,' and all that mental dialogue starts.

When someone asked my teacher Rameshji if any prayer arose for him, he replied, 'God, give me a life where I do not need to ask for anything from anyone, especially from You.' Which, in other words, is the total acceptance of 'what is'. I think it was in Paul Brunton's book *A Search in Secret India*, where he mentioned that he met a leading astrologer of India in those days, in Varanasi. He asked him something to the effect of—'You have mapped out everyone's life, you are so accurate, you are so reputed, but what about your own life? Do you read your own horoscope? And he replied, 'The day I accepted that whatever happens is God's Will, I stopped reading my own chart.'

ACKNOWLEDGEMENTS

Gratitude to my spiritual teacher Ramesh Balsekar and other guides I have had the privilege to meet on life's journey.

My mother Santosh, for her constant guidance and witnessing presence.

My dearest wife Devika, for being my companion on life's journey, through its ups and downs.

My sisters Shibani and Nikki, for gracing my life with their presence and support, and bearing up with my idiosyncracies over the years.

Sangeetha Bhatta, for her help in compiling this list of questions and answers, and working hard in bringing this book to fruition. Natasha Sarkar, for her diligent editing of the book. Saurabh Garge, for the wonderful book cover design.

Girish Jathar, Sanjay Malandkar, Reshma Dalvi, Maniram Pandey and the Yogi Impressions team, for their constant support over the years.

Nikhil Kripalani, Asha Jhaveri, Sangeetha and Eknath Kadam, Roshni Gidwani, Tina Chandan, Nick Arandes, Partha Gálvez and all others who have supported the teaching in various ways—either through offering their time and effort, or through contributions.

'The understanding that
there is no 'other',
but only Consciousness,
transforms relationships.'

For information on Gautam Sachdeva, visit:
www.gautamsachdeva.com

The author may be contacted on email:
info@gautamsachdeva.com

For further details, contact:
Yogi Impressions LLP
1711, Centre 1, World Trade Centre,
Cuffe Parade, Mumbai 400 005, India.

Fill in the Mailing List form on our website
and receive, via email, information on
books, authors, events and more.
Visit: www.yogiimpressions.com

Telephone: (022) 61541500, 61541541
E-mail: yogi@yogiimpressions.com

 Join us on Facebook:
www.facebook.com/yogiimpressions

 Join us on Instagram:
www.instagram.com/yogi_impressions

ALSO BY GAUTAM SACHDEVA

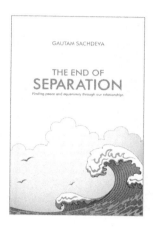

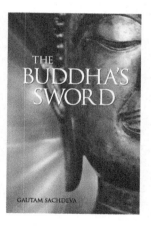

The Sacred India Tarot

Inspired by Indian Mythology and Epics

78 cards + 4 bonus cards + 350 page handbook

The Sacred India Tarot is truly an offering from India to the world. It is the first and only Tarot deck that works solely within the parameters of sacred Indian mythology – almost the world's only living mythology today.

Made in the USA
Coppell, TX
24 July 2021

59308568R00095